50
Kerley Cues
to my
Wonderful Life

50 Kerley Cues to my Wonderful Life

David Kerley

Illustrator Greg Clark

XULON ELITE

Xulon Press
555 Winderley Pl, Suite 225
Maitland, FL 32751
407.339.4217
www.xulonpress.com

© 2024 by David Kerley

All rights reserved solely by the author. The author guarantees all contents are original and do not infringe upon the legal rights of any other person or work. No part of this book may be reproduced in any form without the permission of the author.

Due to the changing nature of the Internet, if there are any web addresses, links, or URLs included in this manuscript, these may have been altered and may no longer be accessible. The views and opinions shared in this book belong solely to the author and do not necessarily reflect those of the publisher. The publisher therefore disclaims responsibility for the views or opinions expressed within the work.

Unless otherwise indicated, Scripture quotations taken from the Holy Bible, New Living Translation (NLT). Copyright ©1996, 2004, 2007 by Tyndale House Foundation. Used by permission of Tyndale House Publishers, Inc.

Paperback ISBN-13: 979-8-86850-333-7
Ebook ISBN-13: 979-8-86850-334-4

To my wonderful wife, Denise,
who fills my heart with joy and laughter
each and every day

and

To my brother of no blood relation, Joshua,
who has walked every step of this journey with me,
in life, theater, baseball, the Bible,
and this little book
of mine

Contents

1	My Wonderful Life Cues	1
2	Treehouse Rescue	7
3	Chicken Neck Delicacy	13
4	Sustaining and Supporting Life	17
5	Aqua Man	21
6	The Smokeless Marlboro Man	25
7	ANYTHING BUT the Kitchen Sink Cliffhanger	31
8	Another Brick in the Wall	37
9	Damsel in Distress	41
10	The Fire Distinguisher—A Beginner's Guide	45
11	Second Class Santa	49
12	The Coat of ANY Color (but Yellow)	53
13	Looking for a Handout	57
14	Beta Club for Dummies	61
15	Where's Nemo? vs. A Whale of a Tale	65
16	Burning Down the Dream House (and Sense of Right and Thong)	71
17	Locked Out or Locked Up (That is the Question)	77
18	Petals and Wings	81
19	Best Boss EVER	87
20	The New Jack Pumpkinhead	91
21	All I Want for Christmas (Came on the Fourth of July)	95

22	I Really Have a Wonderful (Green Room) Life	99
23	Backstage Mama	103
24	Messenger from a Higher Power	109
25	Elliot's Synonym of Homonym	115
26	Another Thing To Be Thankful For	119
27	How I Didn't Meet Andie MacDowell	125
28	Lightning or Stolen Thunder?	129
29	Who IS This Dude by the Name of Ed Block?	133
30	You Must Love Bowling, Huh?	139
31	If a Snake Eats Frequently	143
32	That's a Pretty Good Story!	147
33	But I'm Not an Only Child!	151
34	A Spoonful of Sugar	157
35	Easy Way to Make a Living	163
36	Are You Going to Eat Your Chocolate Cake?	167
37	The Further Away From Home I Feel	171
38	Life Is Just a Leap of Faith	175
39	Take Up Your Cross	179
40	Wandering in the Desert	183
41	Tarawa Backwards	189
42	Many a Strife	193
43	Tradition Permission—and Grace	197
44	It's a Sin to Kill a Mockingbird	201
45	Uncle Dave Scott	205
46	Everyone's Best Friend	209
47	Live Like Saul or Die Like Paul?	213
48	Let Her Who Bore You Rejoice	217
49	Life Is Wonderful	221
50	Transformers	227

An assignment from an online Creative Writing course asked me to rewrite a favorite poem. I chose "If" by Rudyard Kipling.

"When" by David Kerley

When you summon again the courage
To write in poetry or prose,
When you silence the defeats of your past carnage,
But listen to your heart's wishes to still compose.
When your hopes and dreams to give back
Can be coaxed to meet with your foes
Or you stand up to every attack
And shield your precious message from dark shadows.

When you can use your gifts for others' gain,
When you rise to meet the challenge of the day,
When you continue to be thankful and not complain,
And stay on the prescribed and chosen way.
When you can pour new words from an empty vessel,
Or draw beautiful clouds in a vacant sky,
It is the gift and the giver, not you, who is special.
It is your duty to humbly follow and comply.

When you know the right thoughts are inside you,
But you cannot seem to find the exact word,
And your early doubts say all this success is untrue,
You owe it to yourself and to others to persevere undeterred.
When you finally have something that seems to be working
And fear and hesitation conjure apprehension and disbelief,
It is your responsibility, not just your ego, you would be shirking,
When you deny the world, you are only a thief.

When you can persuade that old tenacity to reappear,
When you trust a good editor rather than rewrite the starting block,
When you near the finish line, weary and in low gear,
But still advancing, undaunted and snarling as you beat the clock.
When you see that the lesser book that gets written,
Is always better than the perfect one never published.
When you answer and stand tall—seasoned, steeled, and hard-bitten,
Then, the fruit of your blood, sweat, and tears is no longer rubbish.

"To My Big Brother, George" by Greg Clark Noir Art

My Wonderful Life Cues

Years ago, I was president of our local Jaycee organization. I came up with what I thought was a clever name for the newsletter, a word play around my last name—*Kerley Cues*. Curlicues are decorative curls or twists in calligraphy or in the design of an object. At the time, I thought of cues as words, phrases, or actions in a play or movie that signal a performer to say or do something. A cue is also a prompt or reminder. In slang and as a verb, it means to inform, and give instructions or information.

In preparing this story as an introduction, I learned new definitions and references. Anger cues are warning signs to tell you that you are becoming angry. They can be a physical response, a behavior, a feeling or emotion or a thought. Physical cues are felt in your body, such as feeling warm, sweating, or a rush of energy. Behavioral cues are things you do, such as clenching your teeth, yelling, or slamming doors. Feelings of fear or worry or jealousy, emotional cues, are things you feel. Thought cues are things you think or say to yourself. The way you think about it or interpret an event can increase your anger level and lead to bitter behaviors.

I reflected on how many of the personal stories here are sad or at least negative in some way. My hope was to show their positive points or encourage others rather than the contrary. I was often quick to act on the latter. The words "Wonderful Life" in this book's title refer to one of my favorite films, if not my all-time favorite, *It's a Wonderful Life*. George Bailey was a great man in the eyes of others, but he didn't see that. Undoubtedly, he felt for a long time he had missed out on good fortune. What he didn't realize until he spent some time with Clarence was that his life was important to others, and it was truly wonderful—even the times that maybe weren't so wonderful when they happened.

It took George's life crashing down around him to see what was truly important to him. Yes, at times he was bitter, cynical, cranky, self-centered, but he also sacrificed a lot for his family, friends, and even strangers. So, I'm comparing myself to George with two different perspectives: first, the perspective of negative things that have happened—not as a punishment but a lesson to be learned; secondly, the positive perspective that sometimes you must look hard to find, and don't see for years to come, or are too blind and angry or too hurt to see the bright side at all.

We've all heard the saying, "When life gives you lemons, make lemonade." In the face of adversity or misfortune, we need to encourage optimism and a positive attitude. Sometimes this is easier said than done. When the tough times hit, motivating yourself requires mental strength and often an external push that helps you believe again in the goodness in life.

Maybe it took me over sixty years to learn this, and admittedly, I still need reminders. It is my prayer that you read these stories and are encouraged in some way. Perhaps you will deal with a similar situation more positively. You may have stories from your past that are more challenging or disappointing. Hopefully, you have already, or will begin now to deal with those feelings in a healthy way. And your stories can help you survive and thrive, but more importantly, your stories may help others who are hurting.

Now, for the number 50. It was not the original number of stories from my book. The last week in November 2021, just before my solo performance of the one-person play, *This Wonderful Life* by Steve Murray, God gave me this idea to write these true stories, tying them to *It's a Life Wonderful*, and also scripture. I began to write down notes of memories of my life. In less than forty-eight hours, I had a list of eighty-eight stories, with movie and Bible references. I didn't begin writing until six weeks later. As time went on, I dropped to fifty stories. Just as working on the one-person play, this has been a labor of love. Thank you, Papa, for allowing me to finish it. The number 50 can be found at least 154 times in the Bible. The book of Genesis has fifty chapters. Noah's Ark was fifty cubits wide. The Jubilee year occurs every fifty years. These are my fifty.

Almost everyone knows about the 1946 film by Frank Capra, *It's a Wonderful Life*. Many have seen it, and many watch it at least once every single Christmas. It may not have done particularly well at the box office, but it has grown to be a favorite movie for many. In my book, I want to tell a personal story and then relate it in some way to *It's a Wonderful Life*. Some things I may repeat or list similarly. There may be some comparisons I missed.

For this chapter, comparing *It's a Wonderful Life* to my *50 Kerley Cues*, let us begin with George Bailey—the George Bailey I know and love from Bedford Falls. Of course, I can't leave out another George, the George Bailey of Pottersville who never existed in Bedford Falls. Remember how he felt in his world before Uncle Billy lost the deposit? Remember how he felt when Clarence showed him how people's lives had been affected by his presence and by his absence?

There are dark references in Pottersville, but there are also some in Bedford Falls that seem to be normal. For some people today, their normal may be much worse. They may seem to be coping well on the surface. Others may be distraught like George on that Christmas Eve. You don't have to love *It's a Wonderful Life* to read this book. If you haven't seen it, try this wonderful movie with Jimmy Stewart and Donna Reed . . . I will wait. If there is no desire to watch the movie now, refer to a list of characters and a brief synopsis at the end of this book.

> *This is what the LORD of Heaven's Armies says: Look at what's happening to you! You have planted much but harvest little. You eat but are not satisfied. You drink but are still thirsty. You put on clothes but cannot keep warm.*

Your wages disappear as though you were putting them in pockets filled with holes! (Haggai 1:5–6)

Your word is a lamp to guide my feet and a light for my path. (Psalm 119:105)

Therefore, I will always remind you about these things—even though you already know them and are standing firm in the truth you have been taught. And it is only right that I should keep on reminding you as long as I live. For our Lord Jesus Christ has shown me that I must soon leave this earthly life, so I will work hard to make sure you always remember these things after I am gone. (2 Peter 1:12–15)

All of us must die eventually. Our lives are like water spilled out on the ground, which cannot be gathered up again. But God does not just sweep life away; instead, he devises ways to bring us back when we have been separated from him. (2 Samuel 14:14)

So we tell others about Christ, warning everyone and teaching everyone with all the wisdom God has given us. We want to present them to God, perfect in their relationship to Christ. That's why I work and struggle so hard, depending on Christ's mighty power that works within me. (Colossians 1:28–29)

You can make many plans, but the LORD's purpose will prevail. (Proverbs 19:21)

Cues to Clues to Truths

If my stories of true events are my cues, each has several clues that I didn't always receive or understand fully. In telling these stories, I believe I am finally beginning to listen to God's promises and truths.

#1 God has special plans for our lives.

As God's will unfolds, we know we are here for a reason.

Treehouse Rescue

One Sunday afternoon, I went exploring. As I was only five years old, and Mom and Daddy were getting ready to go to the grocery store, it may not have been the best timing—on their part. Our home was the third one we'd lived in during my young life. We resided in a small cookie-cutter house with a cul-de-sac at the end of the street. My exploration destination that day was just beyond that cul-de-sac.

The other children in our neighborhood had engineered a magnificent abode in the woods. Many casually refer to this creation as a treehouse. We were new to this area, and I didn't have any friends my age. The older kids had yet to recruit me or invite me to see inside their treehouse. I walked to the end of our street, then approached the softwood structure suspended in the hardwood. However, there must have been a shortage of wood because the carpenters had placed the rungs of the ladder too far apart. I was too young and naïve to realize it was by design.

I was a brave explorer, determined and resilient. Even though I had to stretch my legs and arms quite a bit to ascend the ladder, my hard work finally paid off as I entered the forbidden territory. I was relatively new to the exploration business, but my conquest was not as satisfying as I had hoped. Yes, the view of the tiny neighborhood was breathtaking, and the big kids had acquired nice furnishings, but the self-serve Open House tour with no Welcome Wagon didn't take long. I, the daring adventurer, was ready to return to base camp.

The descent proved to be trickier as I couldn't see the next rung below me. My foot searched for it, clawing at the air and finding nothing, so I aborted that mission to troubleshoot this new development. Trying to decide what to do, I got a glimpse of my father at the other end of the street. He was going from door to door, probably asking if anyone had seen his son.

I yelled to let him know where I was. He couldn't hear me yet, but a couple enjoying their backyard did. I would shout, they would look up, and I would hide behind the boards of the tree fortress. I was embarrassed and this seemed to go on for a while, without the curious neighbors figuring out who or what was making all that racket.

As my father got closer to the cul-de-sac, I could see him focus on the "second story" of the large deciduous tree. He knew me well enough to be certain that's where he would find his son. My dad was average height, but as I remember it, he simply reached up and grabbed his young pioneer from within the branches. My arms clung around his neck. I was glad to be liberated from my woodland confinement. Even greater than that, I was elated to be reunited with my brave rescuer—my father. When I leave this world, I know I will see my hero again. I will also see my heavenly Father. When I do, I will shout, "My Daddy, my Daddy! He has come to save me!" just as I did that day in the treehouse.

George Bailey of *It's a Wonderful Life* said he was not a praying man. When there seemed to be no way to solve his problem with the missing eight thousand dollars, he prays in Martini's Bar. Clarence, George's guardian angel, was sent to help him, but George seemed to resist the very help he had asked for. Finally, returning to the bridge where he saved Clarence, he pleads to Clarence and to God. Immediately after praying to God that he wanted to live again, it begins to snow. He is no longer in Pottersville. He is still short eight thousand dollars and will most likely go to jail. He doesn't agonize any further because he returns to the town he always dreamed to escape, and to the once dilapidated, old house on 320 Sycamore he said he wouldn't live in as a ghost, and most importantly, to his wife and four children.

For this is what the Sovereign LORD says: I myself will search and find my sheep. I will be like a shepherd looking for his scattered flock. I will find my sheep and rescue them from all the places where they were scattered on that dark and cloudy day. (Ezekiel 34:11–12)

I myself will tend my sheep and give them a place to lie down in peace, says the Sovereign LORD. I will search for my lost ones who strayed away, and I will bring them safely home again. I will bandage the injured and strengthen the weak. But I will destroy those who are fat and powerful. I will feed them, yes—feed them justice! (Ezekiel 34:15–16)

See, God has come to save me. I will trust in him and not be afraid. The LORD GOD is my strength and my song; he has given me victory." (Isaiah 12:2)

For the LORD your God is living among you. He is a mighty savior. He will take delight in you with gladness. With his love, he will calm all your fears. He will rejoice over you with joyful songs. (Zephaniah 3:17)

For God chose to save us through our Lord Jesus Christ, not to pour out his anger on us. Christ died for us so that, whether we are dead or alive when he returns, we can live with him forever. So encourage each other and build each other up, just as you are already doing. (1 Thessalonians 5:9–11)

For he will rescue you from every trap and protect you from deadly disease. (Psalm 91:3)

Cues to Clues to Truths

#2 Our Father will save us.

When we cry out to Him, He will never fail us in providing shelter, safety, and comfort.

Mom's Locket by Over the Moon Photography

Wedding Day for Don and Nell by Lindsay Barrick

Chicken Neck Delicacy

As long as I can remember, my mother always said her mom's favorite piece of chicken was the neck. I never disputed that but always wondered why that particular piece attracted my grandmother so much. The chicken's neck consists of vertebrae, skin, and stringy, tiny bits of meat. Not many people would go for the neck except to boil them (and several of them) to make soups and gravies. Every time we had chicken, my dear mother would state the one piece of chicken that we never ate was indeed my grandmother's favorite poultry delicacy.

When I was much older, I began to question myself why this was so. My mother wasn't lying. That is what she believed. She saw her mother select that piece at the dinner table. Upon further consideration, I wondered if perhaps my grandmother's objective was to provide for her husband and five children on a small family farm. I believe she knew as well as we do, there just isn't much meat on a neckbone. It may be tasty to some, but would hardly be much of a snack.

I shared this theory with my mom. She saw that maybe I was right. One hen only yields two breasts, two thighs, two legs, two wings, and in this case, one scrawny chicken neck. Eight good pieces of yard bird and a neck for a family of seven. Although it took many years to possibly solve that mystery, I don't believe my grandmother cared in the least. What was important to her was that she fed her family, scrimped to make ends meet, came up with new ideas to make something out of nothing, and wasted not. If her family was loved, nourished, clothed, and safe, then she was happy. She had done her job lovingly. She had done her job well. Come to think of it, maybe my grandmother's favorite piece of the chicken really was the neck!

    I believe Mary Hatch Bailey, George's wife, was caring, clever, hard-working, devoted, and trustworthy. Mary loved the simple life of Bedford Falls, and she deeply loved her family. But just a short while after their wedding ceremony, exchanging vows about "richer or poorer, in sickness and in health," she forfeits the two thousand dollars meant for their honeymoon to calm, at least momentarily, the townspeople after the stock market crashed. I always begrudged the man who insisted he got his full amount of two hundred and forty-two dollars when others took forty or less. Mary's quick thinking and selflessness saved the Bailey Building and Loan that dark day, and most likely the town of Bedford Falls as well. She sacrificed their honeymoon and somehow in only a few hours, turned the old Granville house into a honeymoon cottage.

> *Remember this—a farmer who plants only a few seeds will get a small crop. But the one who plants generously will get a generous crop. You must each decide in your heart how much to give. And don't give reluctantly or in response to pressure. "For God loves a person who gives cheerfully." And God will generously provide all you need. Then you will always have everything you need and plenty left over to share with others.* (2 Corinthians 9:6–8)

> *Then the way you live will always honor and please the Lord, and your lives will produce every kind of good fruit. All the while, you will grow as you learn to know God better and better.* (Colossians 1:10)

> *Taste and see that the Lord is good. Oh, the joys of those who take refuge in him!* (Psalm 34:8)

> *And I am convinced that nothing can ever separate us from God's love. Neither death nor life, neither angels nor demons, neither our fears for today nor our worries about tomorrow—not even the powers of hell can separate us from God's love. No power in the sky above or in the earth below—indeed, nothing in all creation will ever be able to separate us from the love of God that is revealed in Christ Jesus our Lord.* (Romans 8:38–39)

Cues to Clues to Truths

#3 God provides unconditional love.

There isn't anything we have done, should've done, or that's been done to us that can stop Him from loving us.

Sustaining and Supporting Life

As parents, some days are mighty tough. We learn by our mistakes and are encouraged by our successes. In my first marriage, we were returning home from vacation. Like most of us, I needed a vacation after my vacation. It was dinner time, and we were fairly close to home, but not close enough to prepare a meal there.

We stopped at a family restaurant with a buffet. Our older son had a nutritional disorder and would crave certain foods, tastes, and textures like we all do, but often his body couldn't tolerate or benefit well from what went into it. So, the general plan was I would watch both our boys at the table while their mother would get a plate for our older son, take it to him, and then do the same for the younger. Next, their mother would secure her meal and when all three were eating, I could then go to the buffet. That would necessitate Grace be said first.

I hadn't stopped to savor the vacation but simply endured it. My patience was so thin it was transparent. The firstborn child was eating, and the second then received his plate of food. He looked at the plate for a moment, then at me. "What's this?"

I wish I could say I told my little boy the names of every item on his plate and described how they would make him grow to be big, tall, and strong, but I can't. "It's food, nourishment, sustenance. Just eat it." I realize now I probably never used that last big word except in a Sunday school discussion or the telling of this story. My innocent son looked up again at me. "Susta Nuts? Daddy, do I like Susta Nuts? . . . I don't, I don't think I like Susta Nuts." I didn't laugh, but I did start to smile. I realized I was taking my frustration out on my young son, using a word way beyond his years. I was also reminded that God must have a sense of humor, and thankfully He is a God of second chances. Not second chances in the way you might make the same mistake over and over without correction, but He guides us in learning from our mistakes. I wish I could say, too, that this was the only time I spoke without thinking or said something hurtful. If I didn't do so adequately enough then, I now apologize to my son.

On the worst night of George Bailey's life, he returns home to his beautiful family. He yells at Pete about a wreath, complains he isn't a dictionary, chastises Janie's piano music, ignores the fine manners and etiquette of little Tommy, yells at Mary about their daughter's cold, and yells about the drafty, old barn they live in. But despite everything that happened that day, and everything he said in anger to his loved ones, he did manage to regain some patience and care for his daughter, Zuzu. She was sick and only wanted to look at her flower, which George believed caused the cold. When it lost a few petals, she believed with all her heart that her daddy could fix it. Support and sustain what you love.

> *Commit everything you do to the LORD. Trust him, and he will help you. He will make your innocence radiate like the dawn, and the justice of your cause will shine like the noonday sun. Be still in the presence of the LORD, and wait patiently for him to act. Don't worry about evil people who prosper or fret about their wicked schemes.* (Psalm 37:5–7)

> *The LORD is good, a strong refuge when trouble comes. He is close to those who trust in him.* (Nahum 1:7)

Sustaining and Supporting Life

Cues to Clues to Truths

#4 God gives us care and refuge.

He will lead, guide, and direct us if we follow Him. His care will bring us comfort.

Aqua Man

More intelligence doesn't necessarily come with more education or more time, but more experience does provide more opportunities to learn. We can learn through failures and mistakes, perhaps more than we can through successes. I was a Biology major in college. Some classes would include the occasional field trip. I don't remember the particular course, or the lesson of the day, or any experiments we ran, but I do remember one embarrassing thing I did. College was thirty minutes from my home, and I was a commuter.

The field trip's site was a lake near my school of higher learning. I had left my vehicle on campus as we were transported to the lake in vans operated by the college. In class, we had learned what experiments would be carried out and the lessons that would be the supposed outcomes. I was told what we would do on the lake, but I overlooked details that would lead to the lessons on the lake.

We got to the marina as planned and the reverse amphibious assault was launched. We were split into various groups of students to board our assigned vessels. In my defense, let me say before this fateful day I had never embarked on any marine vessel on my own. My prior experience as a sailor consisted of my uncle whisking me up and safely dropping me into his fishing boat. On this same lake, I might add.

A most fortunate lad, I had been grouped with two highly intelligent, attractive females. Being a gentleman, I insisted they board first. I believed the task was a simple one. In hindsight, I wish I had researched nautical scuttlebutt, such as this information expertly explained online by Shawn Buckles.

How to safely board a boat:

Make sure the boat is close to the pier.—After receiving the skipper's permission to board, he or she will pull the boat right alongside the pier or dock. You never want to have to stretch or jump. This could make you lose your balance, which could be potentially dangerous. Wait for the boat to be close enough so you can step on deck without any effort.

Always board near the middle.—Here the boat rocks the least when you place your weight on it, making it easier to keep your balance.

Hold on to the shrouds before placing your foot on deck.—Shrouds are the lines that run alongside the mast to the deck. Always hold on to the shrouds before even thinking about placing your foot on deck. If there are no shrouds, hold on to any lifelines, railing, or the boat itself.

Place your foot and slowly transfer your weight.—The first time you board a boat can be unsettling if you are not prepared. When you place any weight on it, the boat begins to wobble and rock. The smaller the boat, the more it will react to your weight.

Place your second foot only after you have transferred most of your weight.—After your first foot is firmly in place and you have shifted most of your weight onto your front foot, you can begin to move your other foot. Don't let go of the shrouds during all of this.

I saw too late how all this valuable information makes you more confident as a crew member and also increases the confidence that others have in you. I had gallantly allowed the young ladies to board safely, so the boat had moved away slightly from the dock. I wasn't holding on to anything and proceeded with little caution.

With them in the hull and my first foot engaged, the boat rocked heavily. I completely froze with one foot on the boat and one on the dock. I wish I'd remembered about momentum from physics class and carried myself onto the shaky vessel. Since I hesitated, I found myself doing a split and not very gracefully. Soon, I couldn't stretch any more. My flexibility had met its limits and . . . SPLASH!

So, there I was just outside the boat's port side, chest-deep in the reservoir, soaked, and unbelievably embarrassed. Two brave assistants scooped me out of the water, and then cast me into the boat like the whopper that didn't get away.

The rest of the story dealt with being wet and miserable, not only for our excursion, but the journey back to campus and then the ride home. Such is my tale of "the incredible Mr. Limpet." Don Knotts did a much better job.

I fell in a lake, and Clarence jumped in a river. He did that in order to save George after George first saved him. I had to be saved because of my carelessness. Clarence was still an Angel Second Class after a few hundred years. I believe Clarence reading Mark Twain's *The Adventures of Tom Sawyer* had something to do with his plan to save George later, as Tom witnessed his own funeral. Clarence's initial thought was to put himself in jeopardy. George was consumed with suicidal thoughts on the bridge that evening, but he forgot all about that in order to save a stranger.

> *The LORD is more pleased when we do what is right and just than when we offer him sacrifices.* (Proverbs 21:3)

> *If you try to hang on to your life, you will lose it. But if you give up your life for my sake, you will save it.* (Luke 9:24)

> When you go through deep waters, I will be with you. When you go through rivers of difficulty, you will not drown. When you walk through the fire of oppression, you will not be burned up, the flames will not consume you. (Isaiah 43:2)

Cues to Clues to Truths

#5 Our Lord promises us everlasting safety in His hands.

We don't have to panic, and we don't have to run. He will strengthen us in our trials.

The Smokeless Marlboro Man

The Marlboro Man was a figure used in tobacco advertising campaigns for Marlboro cigarettes from 1954 to 1999. From the fictitious American cowboy of those cigarette commercials, we gained a phrase that came to mean, even if in jest, a rugged, self-sufficient, masculine man.

My college years were 1977 to 1981. Many of my friends dipped tobacco. In the Sunday circular, I had found a free coupon for Happy Days. I do not believe it is manufactured any longer, but at the time, United States Tobacco Company (now known as U.S. Smokeless Tobacco Company) made Copenhagen, Skoal, and Happy Days. It was more enticing for me because Harry Gant from my hometown was a NASCAR driver, and his sponsor was Skoal Bandit. Most of my tobacco-experienced friends dipped Copenhagen. Skoal was less strong, and to my friends who had a permanent circle showing in the pocket of every pair of their jeans, Happy Days was like candy.

My father noticed I was preparing to mail off for the free tobacco. A longtime smoker, he said, "Son, you have no business messing with that." I'm certain I carefully explained all the virtues of this transaction. "It's free! Happy Days is part of Harry Gant's sponsor, and my friends tell me it tastes like candy." My father, a Marine and Korean War veteran, gave me the same reply again. I thought I should point out that this would make me more manly, but I finally decided against it.

Soon the small package arrived, and I again heard Dad's Surgeon General warning. In his case, Surgeon Sergeant, but I neglected to follow that Leatherneck's advice. I put a little behind my lip and went outside to mow the yard.

Now, I can't admit I liked it, but I didn't get sick as my father suggested. Probably because it was harmless candy? I didn't stop to question why, since I like candy, but this stuff didn't necessarily grab me right away. Persevering, I thought it deserved another try.

Mom and Dad went to visit relatives a few days later. I had finished my mowing and other chores and was anxious to watch a particular Western I had never seen before. The stage was set. I could sit anywhere on the sofa, or anywhere in the living room for that matter, try a second helping of Happy Days, and watch the movie, having the entire house to myself.

This next part is a little fuzzy, but I do recall settling in to watch the shoot-em-up picture with my new tobacco friend. Unlike the first time, my head immediately began to swim as the cowboy movie credits began to roll. That may not have been the best choice of words because I feel a little queasy.

I had enough wits about me to know I must get that substance out of me. I stood up to go to the restroom, however, I didn't really stand up. I was fixed on the couch although a bit unsteady. Missing the start of the cowboy show, I draped to the floor and then crawled to the bathroom. I disposed of the contraband, patted my face down with cold water, and saw that the reflection in the mirror was white as a ghost. This made sense to me, but I didn't believe ghosts were in quite this much discomfort. Slithering and squirming back to my settee coffin, I laid there waiting to feel better or finally perish, because I knew I was closer to the latter. I missed the entire Old West cowboy story.

My parents returned home. Dad took one look at me and knew what had happened. "Yep! You couldn't listen to dear old Dad. You'll feel better tomorrow." "I don't think I'll make it to tomorrow," I groaned. Needless to say, I did actually live, but I never had the slightest craving for any type of tobacco—dip, snuff, snus, chewing tobacco, plugs, cigars, cigarettes, pipe, or hookah.

Potter had tried many ways to control or stop the Bailey Building and Loan. To ease into this scheme, he first offered George a cigar. He said if George liked it, he would get him a box. Uncle Billy seemed to be more likely to drink alcohol. When people first thought of Uncle Billy, it probably involved his forgetfulness, lackluster work ethic, ability to bumble even the smallest business detail, his array of wildlife, and his dipsomania.

> *Don't act thoughtlessly, but understand what the Lord wants you to do.* (Ephesians 5:17)

> *Don't you realize that your body is the temple of the Holy Spirit, who lives in you and was given to you by God? You do not belong to yourself, for God bought you with a high price. So you must honor God with your body.* (1 Corinthians 6:19–20)

> *And so, dear brothers and sisters, I plead with you to give your bodies to God because of all he has done for you. Let them be a living and holy sacrifice — the kind he will find acceptable. This is truly the way to worship him.* (Romans 12:1)

> *Wine produces mockers; alcohol leads to brawls. Those led astray by drink cannot be wise.* (Proverbs 20:1)

> *Do not carouse with drunkards or feast with gluttons, for they are on their way to poverty, and too much sleep clothes them in rags.* (Proverbs 23:20–21)

> *The temptations in your life are no different from what others experience. And God is faithful. He will not allow the temptation to be more than you can stand. When you*

are tempted, he will show you a way out so that you can endure. (1 Corinthians 10:13)

And this same God who takes care of me will supply all your needs from his glorious riches, which have been given to us in Christ Jesus. (Philippians 4:19)

Cues to Clues to Truths

#6 God will take care of us.

He will do it during the times we need it most, *but* we have to listen to Him when He speaks.

"Pop, I Think You're a Great Guy" by Greg Clark Noir Art

ANYTHING BUT the Kitchen Sink Cliffhanger

In the days when it was safe to leave a child at home in a small town, I once had a memorable Saturday I would've rather forgotten. In that tranquil time of my childhood, the only trouble would most likely come from within. I was to be the source of the trouble that day. I was young, but old enough to know better.

Boys are attracted to adventure and coaxed by danger. I'd watched one of those numerous films in which the protagonist is falling to his death, but at the last fateful second, reaches out to grab a branch protruding from the cliff. It was the branch of safety and salvation.

Those movies are really all alike, but it set this youngster to daydreaming. Daydreams become better when more realistic. Adjourning to the kitchen, I'd reenact the movie's death-defying feat at the most likely place. The branch that would surely save me was Mother's kitchen sink faucet.

As I was plummeting to my supposed death, I reached out for my trusty branch (or kitchen tap). My "woody lifesaver" snapped abruptly, and I was cast down to the depths of the canyon, where black and white tiles checkerboarded our kitchen floor.

That didn't go as I'd expected. Not only was I figuratively dead, but I was also terrified wondering what to do now. Getting up, I quickly replaced the broken, metal branch, and it seemed to take root perfectly. Of course, the only way to see if it worked was to turn on the water. I would give this limb a refreshing and life-giving drink.

I watched in disbelief as the nurturing liquid bubbled and gurgled through the non-certified junior plumber's early work. Since the sneaky solution proved to be faulty, it was time to get serious. My father had taught me about honesty and how George Washington had cut down his father's cherry tree as a youngster. Supposedly, the future Father of Our Country told his father, "I cannot tell a lie. I chopped down the cherry tree." True or not, this may have been the story of Washington I knew best.

My father was a Marine. He taught me much, particularly in the years to come. Those lessons seemed to have only landed with me in the latter decades. Dad was a great teacher who had a poor student. His first lesson, and a constant one, was to do the right thing, in the right way, for the right reasons. Inspired by that early lesson, I quietly told my father when he returned home, "I cannot tell a lie. I cut down Mom's sink faucet." Next, the modern Master George braced for his punishment.

The reader should now be learning about the harsh paddling I received. Instead, we loaded up in the old Oldsmobile, after Dad's sixth day in a row of working to feed his family—to go to the hardware store—and spend money promised to other needs to repair my error in judgment.

I may not have learned much about plumbing that Saturday afternoon, but I was being taught a larger lesson. My father was the biggest man in town. The biggest heart I knew repaired the damaged sink as his lucky apprentice tried to learn how to replace a faucet. I am sixty-four years old (this many, flashing both hands six times and then holding up only four fingers), and to do what my dad did, I would have to watch a YouTube video a dozen times. Honestly, the real lesson, the lifelong lesson, had nothing to do with plumbing.

As children, we all dream of what we want to become someday. I hope many achieve those dreams, but realistically few offspring do. As young teens, we may wish to excel at a particular sport or to simply be popular. When we graduate to the real world, we're constantly searching for the dream job to buy that dream house, dream car, and then have the dream family. If you only wish it to be true, unfortunately, you'll be disappointed. Life just doesn't cooperate that way.

Everyone should have goals. In the Jaycees, I learned that *goals* are the gameplan of achieving life's successes. From the College of Hard Knocks, I learned if you fail to plan, you plan to fail. All of us should have a dream, but it isn't enough just to simply have that dream. You need to work at it. Cultivate it. That also means you must define and redefine what it is exactly that you want to do, what you want to achieve, and all that is great.

The bottom line for all of us should be, more than anything else, to be the best person we can be. That is what my father wanted to teach me on that Saturday afternoon, and every day of his life. My father was so special, he has kept on teaching me even after he died. I suppose many people would look at my great failures and minor successes, and declare I didn't listen to my father or follow his instructions in the slightest. Seeing the big picture though, I hope I am a good person. I trust there are more examples of me doing good than the alternative. Since retirement, I often understand there are more failures than anything else.

Then, I remember that corrected failures are the real purpose, and that the true target of being a good person is to do the right thing in the right way for the right reasons. If I feel I am losing sight of that, the way to get back on track is to ask myself what my father might have done in this situation. It seems to have taken me a lifetime to choose to act only out of kindness, compassion, and love, like my father.

I didn't save myself that Saturday morning. Neither did George Washington in my opinion. My father saved me, not by using the feeble branch from the cliff, but by extending his own hand and sowing his wisdom. I suppose the rooting of his work is up to me. My father saved me that day, and many days before and since by teaching me this, "You will never go wrong when you do what's right."

I remember an old joke that was similar to the George Washington myth. A boy was looking for excitement on his family's farm. He wondered if he was strong enough to push over the outhouse. He was surprised to watch it tumble down the hill, but bored quickly and set out to find more mischief. When his father caught up with him, he asked if he had anything to tell him about their outdoor plumbing facilities. The young son chose the George Washington route as did I and confessed. Then, his father spanked him severely. After his tears subsided, he asked his father why he didn't treat him the same way George Washington's father treated his son? He answered, "Because George Washington's father wasn't in that cherry tree when it came down!"

Peter Bailey asked his older son on the night he was to die, "You wouldn't mind coming back to the Building and Loan, would you?" George didn't want to at all. He could have agreed out of guilt, or a desire to pay a debt to his father, but I think what stuck with him most was how his father taught him to deal with demanding situations. "Pop, you want a shock? I think you're a great guy." A sign hanging in Peter Bailey's office after his death reads, "All you can take with you is that which you've given away."

> *And you must commit yourselves wholeheartedly to these commands that I am giving you today. Repeat them again and again to your children. Talk about them when you are at home and when you are on the road, when you are going to bed and when you are getting up. Tie them to your hands and wear them on your forehead as reminders. Write them on the doorposts of your house and on your gates. (Deuteronomy 6:6–9)*

> *The LORD is like a father to his children, tender and compassionate to those who fear him. (Psalm 103:13)*

> *No, O people, the LORD has told you what is good, and this is what he requires of you: to do what is right, to love mercy, and to walk humbly with your God. (Micah 6:8)*

So let us come boldly to the throne of our gracious God. There we will receive his mercy, and we will find grace to help us when we need it most. (Hebrews 4:16)

Cues to Clues to Truths

#7 God promises us help in time of need.

No one understands our pain better than Jesus. We can come to God asking for mercy, grace, help, and forgiveness.

Another Brick in the Wall

You are correct. This title is a song from Pink Floyd. Upon hearing the lyrics for the first time, one may think they are saying education is unnecessary. If a wall already exists between teacher and pupil, then any injustice can only add another brick. Perhaps we aren't trying to reach students that skillfully or effectively enough. If a student, or even our own child, questions or rebels, maybe our best plan would be to refrain from saying, "Hush up!" and say instead, "Hold on, that is a good point. Let's talk about that." This story is less about Pink Floyd and more about brick masonry. Before I get to that, I need to give some background first.

Many years earlier, a drunk driver had taken down a smaller portion of a retaining wall at my parents' home. Every summer after that, my father and I were content to mow around the broken edge of the wall and also the small pile of whole or shattered bricks from that crash that had been moved to the basement door.

Fast forward a couple of decades. I was now a father, but my wife and I had separated. I was mowing my parents' lawn one weekend when I had my son. He was inside drawing or playing video games. I finished my chore, then I announced we were going to repair that wall. Father and son set out for the hardware store for supplies.

I'd never had any instruction on laying brick, but I felt I had the general idea. We headed back home with our supplies to begin the planning phase. This part went fairly well by knocking away the old mortar from the bricks and salvaging any whole bricks and pieces if large enough. Since we couldn't use all the original bricks, we redesigned for a more narrow and shorter section of the tapered wall. Next, we mixed our mortar and got to business. I did realize I was expected to set up a string line for bricklaying, but I believed it was unnecessary due to its small size.

The next thing I knew, it was getting dark. Diligently, I pulled the car down to the other entrance of the property to shine some light on the subject. We finally finished, proud of our accomplishment.

The next day, we walked out to inspect our masterpiece. The string line I had skipped caused some waviness in the structure. The mortar I had mixed proved to be too soupy, and although it would set up well enough over time, we had dripped some of it on places that should be free of mortar.

That evening, I returned my son to his home. His mother asked, "What did you and your dad do this weekend?" "We built a wall," he replied. I honestly believed this was the first time she was impressed. "Wow! You built a wall? What did you learn?" Before I could explain it was only a small repair and there was no actual, full-length wall built, my son answered his mother's question. And I quote: "I learned not to do it in the dark." Who can argue with that?

If your only experience of parenting comes from the movies, you may think it an easy task. George and Mary Bailey were excellent parents who loved their children very much. Though it's quite understandable that on December 24 that year, George had a little more on his mind.

He snapped at three of his children who only wanted their father's help and attention on the most thrilling night of the year. Janie practiced her piano for the party that evening, but Mr. Bailey was irritated by the noise. Pete needed spelling assistance with the Christmas story he was writing, and little Tommy was learning burp etiquette.

After all that, George went upstairs to check on Zuzu, sick in bed with a cold. She had been given a flower at school for a prize. She didn't want to crush it, so she didn't button her coat. Little Miss Zuzu loved her flower so much, even though it was shedding petals and was the cause of her current malady, that she only wanted to gaze at her flower instead of going to sleep.

Her father was at the top of his game at this point, being so caring, devoted, and sensitive with his younger daughter. Why couldn't he have had the same type of reaction with Janie's music, Pete's story, and Tommy's tiny belch no one heard but him? His behavior was bad enough, and then he had to yell at his daughter's teacher on the phone and demolish his full-scale models of skyscrapers and suspension bridges.

> *For you are all children of the light and of the day; we don't belong to darkness and night. So be on your guard, not asleep like the others. Stay alert and be clearheaded.* (1 Thessalonians 5:5–6)

> *Fathers, do not provoke your children to anger by the way you treat them. Rather, bring them up with the discipline and instruction that comes from the Lord.* (Ephesians 6:4)

> *The LORD says, "I will guide you along the best pathway for your life. I will advise you and watch over you.* (Psalm 32:8)

Cues to Clues to Truths

#8 Our God will teach us.

He who knows all things promises to be our personal counselor.

Damsel in Distress

My first home was with my parents on Ivanhoe Avenue in Asheville, North Carolina. We lived there approximately three years before moving to Bear Creek Road in the same city. The second location was further out of town, but both places had hills and woods nearby to play.

On Ivanhoe, I was too young yet to know of Sir Walter Scott's fictional Saxon knight of the same name. His allegiance to King Richard and love for Lady Rowena damaged his relationship with his father. His father disinherited him, and Ivanhoe had to find a respectable way to reenter society. In the novel, there is a tournament, a Black Knight, an appearance by Robin Hood, disguises, castles, witchcraft accusations, and marriage. I did not know the book or its story at the time, so I cannot blame what happened to me on *Ivanhoe*.

Dad was at work (sales for a cigarette company) and Mom was cleaning our home and preparing a delicious meal. An only child, I was playing in our yard, so Mother thought. I had been playing there but seemed to have wandered off. Of course, I had no way of knowing, but my poor mother, Nell, was terrified. When it came to dangers, hazards, and peril of all kinds, Mom's imagination was much more active than mine would ever be, on any topic. And I may have neglected to state that behind that property was a steep bank she would call a cliff and below it were train tracks.

Mom went to my room to check on me, just in case, then to the yard, but I was nowhere to be found. So I must be on the railway, tied there by desperadoes like some woman in danger. And lest we not forget, the steaming locomotive approacheth! Remember, I said she had an active imagination when it came to natural disasters, sinister plots, and transportation accidents, especially those concerned with firstborn and only heir to the throne of worry.

My poor mother was the damsel in distress that day. I assume she ran through the woods, arms flailing, screeching my name just to peer over the canyon's edge (seriously, it was only a bank) to dreadfully glimpse at the remains of her wonderful, yet foolish son.

Alas, the *3:10 to Yuma* on its way to haul murderer and stagecoach robber, Glenn Ford, to justice had not made its way there yet. Lucky for her, and me, but the fact remained her baby boy was still missing. Maybe Ford's gang had taken her unfortunate offspring hostage?

Of course, none of those notions were true, and I'd been momentarily led astray by my first pretty face. The little girl who lived two houses down the street had innocently invited me to play at her home. I was completely safe at all times, and Mother was so happy to discover me without a scratch and whisked me off to Rapunzel's tower, complete with a moat and a congregation of bloodthirsty alligators. "Home Sweet Home."

Some say that *It's a Wonderful Life* and *A Christmas Carol* are the same story. Although there may be similarities, I do not buy into that entirely. Clarence takes George to the fictitious alternate town of Pottersville. Scrooge has a string of ghostly visitors.

The outcomes are Ebenezer is miraculously transformed into a kinder, gentler man and Mr. Bailey is shown that he really did have a wonderful life. Sure, he may have to go to jail over the missing eight thousand dollars while the guilty culprit in a wheelchair casually returns to his hideout. Similarly, they both benefit from their individual blindness being lifted. George is returned to his loving family, and Ebenezer embarks upon a new life of caring and virtue.

> *When he arrives, he will call together his friends and neighbors, saying, 'Rejoice with me because I have found my lost sheep.' In the same way, there is more joy in heaven*

over one lost sinner who repents and returns to God than over ninety-nine others who are righteous and haven't strayed away! (Luke 15:6–7)

Those who know your name trust in you, for you, O LORD, do not abandon those who search for you. (Psalm 9:10)

You will keep in perfect peace all who trust in you, all whose thoughts are fixed on you! (Isaiah 26:3)

Cues to Clues to Truths

#9 God promises perfect peace in Him.

No matter how difficult a situation is, we should keep trusting God. More than just peace of mind, it will be a perfect peace.

The Fire Distinguisher—A Beginner's Guide

Fire is a monster. It destroys forests, damages homes and lives, eradicates clothing, furniture, collections, and mementoes. It chokes life, discerning no difference in flora or fauna. It consumes.

Yet fire is also a friend. In the forest, it can remove underbrush, clean debris from its floor, and open the environment to sunlight. In a human environment, it can be a means to feed a hungry child or warm a shivering traveler. It can also scar and cripple.

Maybe what defines the duality of fire depends on what does or doesn't confine it. A blaze left uncontrolled seeks out increased fuel until all is consumed or is extinguished. The journey from the ignition of tinder, kindling, and firewood to smoke and later ashes, fans the flames that distinguish between burning questions and fiery judgments.

Illuminating perhaps the fiery furnace of Shadrach, Meshach, and Abednego, the smoking fire pot and flaming torch of Abram to Abraham, and the burning bush of Moses that although it was on fire, it did not burn up, these are all symbols of God's miraculous energy, sacred light, brilliant radiance, and the burning heart of purity, love, and clarity.

However, by sharing so much light on Smokey the Bear academia and biblical truth, I've ignored the very spark which ignited the flames of my interest. I did refer to this as a beginner's guide after all.

In the spacious backyard of my second home in only four years of life, I experienced it for the first time and was attracted like a moth to my own burning bush. The original represents God's intention to destroy sin and dispense the grace. My burning bush wasn't really a bush at all, but I see six decades later that it may have been the same lesson. I was just too young to understand it fully.

One Saturday, Dad set out to grill burgers and hot dogs. During the process of lighting the coals and preparing everything from the charcoal itself to the intended sacrifices, my father kept me safely away while I played. When he returned to our kitchen briefly, I thought I would help my father and at the same time, I would investigate this new fascination of mine, fire. I had been lit.

Having not yet entered the halls of education, I still absolutely knew that fire gave heat and light. The fire was hot, even hotter than the weather that day. The roaring fire would soon be cooking our burgers and roasting our hot dogs. Although it would have been easier to notice in the dark, I could still see how glowing embers released the sparkling, shimmering flames that danced above the grate. I gazed at the fire my father had built, mesmerized by the array of colors before me. I knew that the reds, oranges, yellows, whites, and blues were all fire. Above the blaze, I observed something, yet invisible, that made the trees in the distance appear blurry and squiggly. I had no idea what that was. So, I stuck a broom in it!

As it turns out, that squirmy stuff is fire, too. Who knew? My brave father arrived just in time to rescue me and douse the burning broom.

The only time I remember any fire at all in *It's a Wonderful Life*, it must be when George, as a boy and a young man, made a wish by the antique cigar lighter at Gower's Drug Store. He grabbed the lighter and said, "I wish I had a million dollars!" After the sparks came from the lighter, he would shout, "Hot dog!"

There was plenty of freezing water, ice, and snow at times but no fire other than the lighter and lit cigars. Similar to my father's jumping to my aid, George jumped in the freezing, black water to rescue Harry, and years later, Clarence.

The Fire Distinguisher–A Beginner's Guide

For God has not given us a spirit of fear and timidity, but of power, love, and self-discipline. (2 Timothy 1:7)

*When you dig a well,
you might fall in.
When you demolish an old wall,
you could be bitten by a snake.
When you work in a quarry,
stones might fall and crush you.
When you chop wood,
there is danger with each stroke of your ax.
Using a dull ax requires great strength,
so sharpen the blade.
That's the value of wisdom;
it helps you succeed.* (Ecclesiastes 10:8–10)

The LORD is good, a strong refuge when trouble comes. He is close to those who trust in him. But he will sweep away his enemies in an overwhelming flood. He will pursue his foes into the darkness of night. (Nahum 1:7–8)

Then if my people who are called by my name will humble themselves and pray and seek my face and turn from their wicked ways, I will hear from heaven and will forgive their sins and restore their land. (2 Chronicles 7:14)

Cues to Clues to Truths

#10 Our God promises forgiveness of our sins.

He will answer our prayers when we humble ourselves, and seek Him.

"Excuse Me, Excuse Me" by Greg Clark Noir Art

Second Class Santa

In my older age, I've enjoyed acting and directing in community theater. I wanted to get involved earlier, but I was afraid to audition. There's also a darker secret that I've tried to keep hidden. So much so that I tell people my first play was *The Wizard of Oz* when I was forty-seven. I had hoped to play the Cowardly Lion but was cast as the Wizard, the "star" of the show.

My deep, dark secret confession is that my first play actually was in the first grade. It was a Christmas presentation by the first and second grades of my elementary school. It wasn't so much a play really as there was no script, but more like a musical with me as the sole non-singing actor. Sounds exciting, doesn't it?

Lucky for me, I was the only Husky jean-wearing male student in both grades. So, acting prowess aside, I was unanimously cast as that jolly iconic figure, Santa. In college, I would become afraid of the aspect of auditions and was spared this in my true debut as a thespian. Everyone else in the classes' program were to be singers, regardless of their singing ability. "Hey, Mrs. Ingram! I can make a joyful noise, too!"

The premise unfolded with the two teachers selecting the Christmas songs to be presented and playing the music. My castmates had to learn many lyrics. They would need no choreography since they would carol chorus style. I don't remember any of their selections, but I do know that one of the songs spoke of leaving snacks out for Santa Claus. Cruel, don't you think? —That every household would leave high-calorie sweets and cookies to be washed down with milk or eggnog for Santa, who everyone knows has a weight problem. And yes, me as well.

So, I had no lines to memorize as the crooners were my storytellers. I wasn't much more than a mime with props. How difficult could that be? Blocking was my assignment, which is the precise staging of actors in order to facilitate the performance of a play, ballet, film or opera. While the others learned the songs, I was briefly told what to do and when to do it. Piece of cake, right? Sorry, no calorie puns for Mr. Claus.

Mrs. Ingram and Mrs. Moose built the fireplace, which I would enter from stage left, out of cardboard boxes and covered them in paper that resembled bricks. On top of the fireplace mantle were construction paper candles, taped to the fireplace with small pieces of cellophane tape on only one side of each candle. I had a red and white Santa suit and a Santa mask with a cap attached. The teachers decided I wasn't quite fat and jolly enough, so they stuffed my suit with pillows.

Earlier, I mentioned a song about a snack for Santa. I have no idea what possessed Mrs. Ingram to get actual snacks and actual Coca-Cola. Okay, so maybe it was all right to have a bottle of soda, but why in the world would she open it? I couldn't drink anything with the mask in place because there was no opening for the mouth. The two slits for eyes were almost nonexistent.

Showtime! Everyone's parents and families were seated in the gymnatorium. The music selections were going nicely while Saint Nick waited for his cue. The cue came and Santa magically left the North Pole and instantly appeared in this three-sided, one-room house through its chimneyless fireplace of combustible products.

The fireplace seemed to be large enough, but the opening proved otherwise, especially with the extra padding for chubby Santa Claus. The blinded Santa came forth and stepped on the plate of cookies. This wasn't obvious but knocking over the uncapped Coke bottle certainly was. Having emerged from the cardboard brick cocoon, the inevitable rustling sent the colored paper candles flailing in many directions. Santa tripped on his red pant legs that weren't hemmed properly and stumbled backwards, crushing the cardboard boxes. I mean the fireplace.

If the audience hadn't noticed the cookie trampling and soft drink spilling, or even the zigzagging candles, it would have been impossible to miss the reverse dive to flatten the firebox from mantle to hearth. "That was so funny! Will you be our Santa next year, too?" Me: "Snow thanks!" My next play was not until forty-one years later. Clarence, Angel Second Class, would've willingly taken the plunge.

George Bailey proved to be a much better sport than me when he and Mary danced backwards into the swimming pool at the high school dance. Everyone joined in—kids in their tuxes and prom gowns, even the principal. I believe George and Mary actually won the Charleston contest! Afterwards, he borrowed a football uniform and robe from the locker room to replace their wet clothes. They walked home singing "Buffalo Gals," and George offered to lasso the moon.

> *Each time he said, "My grace is all you need. My power works best in weakness." So now I am glad to boast about my weaknesses, so that the power of Christ can work through me.* (2 Corinthians 12:9)

> *Don't be afraid, for I am with you. Don't be discouraged, for I am your God. I will strengthen you and help you. I will hold you up with my victorious right hand.* (Isaiah 41:10)

Cues to Clues to Truths

#11 God will lift us up.

God is in control, and He tells us to put our faith in Him.

The Coat of ANY Color (but Yellow)

Undoubtedly, you've heard of the Bible's coat of many colors. Jacob, who had several sons and favoring one, gave Joseph the coat as a gift. The other brothers envied him, seeing the special coat as a sign that Joseph would assume leadership of the family.

Dolly Parton's song, "Coat of Many Colors," musically paints a beautiful story of Dolly's mother making a coat from many different rags to keep her daughter warm. In the lyrics, the mother tells about Joseph's coat and suggests the new coat will bring good luck and happiness. At school, her classmates laugh at her, and she explains what her Mama had told her while she was sewing the coat. The young students didn't understand. Her song ends with the young daughter realizing a person is only poor if they choose to be. In her coat of many colors, she believed she was as rich as possible.

Knowing these two stories, it pains me to tell this story of my youth. We were not wealthy by any means, but I came to realize much later that we had what we had because my parents worked hard, saved every penny they could, planned wisely, and spent what little money was left as responsibly as they knew how. I know now they made sacrifices for me. They wanted me to have a much better life than they had.

Before I started school, my wonderful parents scrimped and saved to buy me a raincoat. I couldn't wait for my education to begin and hoped the weatherman would say I needed my beautiful raincoat every day. School started, and I entered the first grade. The weather was bright and sunny. My opinion of school was a little more dreary. Finally, the day came when I most definitely needed my bright yellow coat.

My yellow slicker and I boarded the yellow school bus that rainy morning. I proudly wore the reward of my parents' penny-pinching, dry as a bone while other children were drenched and soaked. I didn't dare say anything about their watery predicament.

Maybe they needed something or someone to laugh at like the children in Dolly's song. Maybe they were like Joseph's jealous brothers. A couple older kids started picking on me about my yellow raincoat. Before long, everyone else chimed in, too.

"Is that a lemon, a banana, or a squash?" "I think this shower is about over because the *sun* just came out!" "Quack, quack!" "What is a taxicab doing on a school bus?" "Hey, mustard! Where's the ketchup?" "What in the world? It's a school bus riding a school bus!" "I guess this school bus just had a baby!" Then, the knock-knock joke: "Knock, knock?" "Who's there?" "Hurricane." "Hurricane who?" "Hurry! Cane you find him an *uglier* raincoat to wear?" "Impossible!" Oh, it was a fun day! It was a fun day all the way around. I wish I could say I saw the humor in it, that those jokes were mine, like Steve Martin in *Roxanne*, making fun of his own large nose.

I know what Joseph experienced, being sold into Egypt, was much worse than what happened to me that soppy day. It would make me feel good if I forgave them then as Joseph did his brothers.

I want to say I had the wisdom of little Dolly Parton. That I was patient with them, understood them, listened quietly to the ridiculers, and then with nothing but kindness in my heart, told them about my parents' sacrifices in loving me so very much they did without to provide for me. They not only provided the coat of any yellowish color, but Mom and Dad's golden love for their son gleamed brighter than the sun, not just the yellow garment.

At the end of the day, I carried the lemon-colored coat home, hung it in my closet and never wore it again, no matter how many times my mom brought it out or feared that I would be uncomfortable from the weather or become sick. It didn't matter to me how many pennies she had saved or tears she had cried.

The coat of cowardice was more painful than the trench coat I was given. I was the true yellow thing that day, more yellow than the raincoat. More cowardly and faint of heart. More lily-livered and chicken-hearted than *any* yellow thing. More cowardly, resentful, and grudging than the envious, soggy bus riders in the storm.

I was the yellow varmint in the yellow garment, the yellowbelly inside the yellow jacket, and that really stings me to this day. This concludes the story of the worst school bus ride I ever had. The runner-up was the day Bus #33 wrecked.

Children can be cruel. Violet Bick may have been a flirtatious young lady, but she certainly had feelings. Stepping into her shoes for a moment, I wonder why she planned to move to New York as an adult. I wonder why she ended up staying in Bedford Falls after all. Maybe in the Big Apple, she could start over with a clean slate? Pick up and do it all over again, but this time, a little wiser. Perhaps she stayed because of the courage George's story gave her. Was it the hope that those same townspeople would also care for her like they did for George? Or was it the realization it was time to do something about herself, not simply change locations or run away from the problem?

> *No, dear brothers and sisters, I have not achieved it, but I focus on this one thing: Forgetting the past and looking forward to what lies ahead, I press on to reach the end of the race and receive the heavenly prize for which God, through Christ Jesus, is calling us.* (Philippians 3:13–14)
>
> *For God has not given us a spirit of fear and timidity, but of power, love, and self-discipline.* (2 Timothy 1:7)
>
> *So be strong and courageous! Do not be afraid and do not panic before them. For the LORD your God will personally go ahead of you. He will neither fail you nor abandon you."* (Deuteronomy 31:6)

> *But those who trust in the LORD will find new strength. They will soar high on wings like eagles. They will run and not grow weary. They will walk and not faint.*
> (Isaiah 40:31)

Cues to Clues to Truths

#12 God will renew our strength.

Part of being strong and having courage means trusting in the Lord as our true source of strength. He can give us strength to soar over everything else and strength to move forward.

Looking for a Handout

A handout can be a few different things. It refers to a folder or circular of information to be distributed freely. It may mean a prepared statement which is released to the news media. I most often think of it as a portion of food, clothing, or money given to someone who desperately needs it.

I remember so often my father giving to others who were less fortunate. Not just money, but he also gave goods or his time. He took clothes to a needy family. He bought a meal for poor individuals more than a few times. He gave away to those who needed it more, but he also gave to those who asked for it, whatever it was.

When I was in school, my father was known as "The Tom's Man." He sold Tom's snacks—cheese crackers, potato chips, candy and the like. Some people even thought his name *was* Tom. People would ask for samples, and Dad would hand them out. I thought that was absurd. Who hasn't tasted a cheese cracker or a peanut? They know how good they are! If they want one so badly, why can't they pay for it?

I also remember when I was a little boy standing by a friend who was one year younger than me. Someone handed the young fellow a crisp dollar bill. I held out my little hand but received no money. I was told, "No, you have a father." Well, yes, I did have a father—a great father! If I didn't though, I knew you couldn't buy one with a single dollar bill. I was sorry my friend only had one parent. I wasn't bitter about what happened that day, but it has stuck with me for sixty years.

Later, as a young man with a family, I remember driving to a meeting in Advance, North Carolina. My day included an overheated radiator only a few miles away from my destination and a few minutes from my appointment. This was in the ancient times of no cellphones for anyone and no credit card for me.

I remember well the location where my car broke down. I can't pass that place without thinking about this story. There was a rural service station within walking distance. I set out in hopes of finding my Good Samaritan.

The owner and mechanic did come to my rescue. I had no credit card and very little cash. Fervently promising to send him a check as soon as I got home, I'm certain the nice gentleman believed I was taking advantage of him.

Nevertheless, the skilled technician determined the reason for the overheating, repaired it, and bid me farewell. I had unfortunately missed my meeting and headed home. As soon as I got in the house, I wrote a check, one that thankfully wouldn't bounce, and addressed it to the man who rescued me on the side of the road. I feel certain he was shocked to receive his payment.

In my life since those two stories, I have dealt with many a beggar and panhandler. Some I treated like my helping hand mechanic treated me. Others got no good neighbor treatment. Without a doubt, I am sure my kind heart was misused many times, but I also suspect that my cold heart sometimes made the wrong decision.

Did I reason who I felt deserved the helping hand and who didn't? How did I begin to do such a judgmental thing? Were my decisions judicious or selfish? I suspect my judicious conclusions rendered some sort of aid, whether it be money, food, goods, or a ride somewhere. Maybe that means that my selfish answers were likely, "No." Whether I was wrong or right has more to do with whether I slept well that night. If I did something good and was only duped, my heart was in the right place. Even if I was wrong to contribute, I think my heart was in the right place at the right time.

Was Harry's life more special or precious than George's? Harry was the football star, went to college, and received the Medal of Honor.

Looking for a Handout

George also did honorable acts, especially under more private circumstances and most certainly with restraints on his own life, curtailing his dreams. Harry seemed to be living the dream. On the other hand, George dreamed for a particular way to live and never felt his way was much of a living until Clarence came into his life. In their own ways, both Bailey boys lived their lives to the fullest. A spectacular life in a plain, brown wrapper is in many ways more wonderful than any other. Helping others actually helps yourself. Edwin Markham wrote, "There is a destiny which makes us brothers; no one goes his way alone. All that we send into the lives of others comes back into our own." My father had it right all along.

> *Don't worry about anything; instead, pray about everything. Tell God what you need, and thank him for all he has done. Then you will experience God's peace, which exceeds anything we can understand. His peace will guard your hearts and minds as you live in Christ Jesus.* (Philippians 4:6–7)
>
> *You can make many plans, but the LORD's purpose will prevail.* (Proverbs 19:21)
>
> *Give all your worries and cares to God, for he cares about you.* (1 Peter 5:7)
>
> *For you will be treated as you treat others. The standard you use in judging is the standard by which you will be judged.* (Matthew 7:2)
>
> *Oh, the joys of those who are kind to the poor! The LORD rescues them when they are in trouble. The LORD protects them and keeps them alive. He gives them prosperity in the land and rescues them from their enemies.* (Psalm 41:1–2)

> *You must each decide in your heart how much to give. And don't give reluctantly or in response to pressure. "For God loves a person who gives cheerfully." And God will generously provide all you need. Then you will always have everything you need and plenty left over to share with others.* (2 Corinthians 9:7–8)

Cues to Clues to Truths

#13 God is the ultimate cheerful giver.

God delights in giving to us. He desires to see us give with the same good heart, emphasizing charity with intention.

Beta Club for Dummies

Before getting your feathers ruffled, know that I mean no disrespect. This educational youth organization recognizes high academic achievement, rewarding and nurturing worthy character, fostering leadership skills and encouraging service to others. Its only dummy I know was "yours truly."

I had been in Beta Club for a year, and it was time to induct our new members. This was a solemn, dignified ceremony for which the entire student body was present in the high school's gymnasium, filling bleachers on both sides. The lights were dimmed to offer assurance of noble and lofty promises of royal regality.

Current members, draped in retired graduation robes, were strategically placed at the foot of Bleacher Mountain, one Beta per each section. To add an exalted touch, we held candles, shining light out of the darkness. Our mission was to escort the conscripts individually to the podium as each name was announced. They would stand up when they heard their name in the roll call and make their way to the Beta Club member assigned to their section, weaving and stumbling between the seated students. Then, the escort and new companion walked almost Wedding March style to their celebrated destination.

I certainly understood budget cuts, but certain diminishments are inexcusable. My candelabrum or candle holder was created with a 3" by 3" piece of construction paper. The last time I checked, construction paper was flammable. It may have been suitable if careful and meticulous trimming to the center yielded a perfectly matching opening for the circumference of the candle. As far as candlesticks go, I was stuck!

Again, with the budget downsizing, my minuscule remains of a candle must've been handed down from many initiations past. Our candles were lit. We walked to our stations, and the ceremony began.

My embarrassing piece of paraffin was burning at an accelerated rate. With the nimble hands of a casino dealer, I carefully pushed the candlewick up above the construction paper, hot molten wax dripping to my left palm through the gaping hole that had been violently poked through my flimsy, colored 3" by 3" piece of construction paper.

I was thankful I could leave my little candle a bit more burning room. I silently prayed none of the initiates would be seated in my section. Knowing what I know now, I absolutely wish I had blown out my tiny light of education and stood there quietly in the dark. But my assignment must be carried out exactly as I was ordered. I did wish we were outfitted with flashlights, but how could the club afford the expensive batteries?

It became increasingly apparent that I only had about one or two good pushes left on my candle. Desiring this silly ceremony would burn out, I mean end, I gingerly extended the candle's bite-sized bit once more, and that is when my worst fears were realized. The flimsy paper candle holder, which was now soaked through with hot wax, burst into flames!

I had been taught at an early age if my clothes caught fire I should, "stop, drop, and roll." Unfortunately, I had not been advised what to do if actually holding a ball of fire. I remembered blowing out candles on my birthday cake. I tried that approach but the draft only fanned the flames. Don't forget that I was wearing a robe with flowing sleeves.

My next brilliant idea was to fling the whole thing to the floor and stomp on it. Now, stomping on the floor of a quiet gym makes quite a racket. If no one had previously noticed what was happening, they definitely did when I danced the firelighter boogie. And if there are three Ps of fire safety, I vote for Prevent and just forget about Plan and Practice. Smokey the Bear would be so proud. "Only you can prevent foolish fires," pleaded the human torch.

Don't pick on poor Clarence for failing to earn his wings for almost three hundred years. He was happy to help in any way he could. Earning his wings was not the only reason or incentive. Clarence had hope. If Clarence ever felt beat down and defeated, he was not yet consumed. There was still a remnant with a promise of restoration. Clarence knew the Lord's mercies and compassions. No matter how bad the past day or past assignment was, Clarence knew he could look to a new morning with faith and hope.

> *Yet I still dare to hope when I remember this: The faithful love of the LORD never ends! His mercies never cease. Great is his faithfulness; his mercies begin afresh each morning.* (Lamentations 3:21–23)

> *Dear brothers and sisters, when troubles of any kind come your way, consider it an opportunity for great joy. For you know that when your faith is tested, your endurance has a chance to grow. So let it grow, for when your endurance is fully developed, you will be perfect and complete, needing nothing.* (James 1:2–4)

> *Trust in the Lord with all your heart; do not depend on your own understanding. Seek his will in all you do, and he will show you which path to take.* (Proverbs 3:5–6)

Cues to Clues to Truths

#14 God will make our paths straight.

Through His righteousness and wisdom, we will be able to make the right decisions and be wise when faced with confusion.

"Captain Nemo" by Greg Clark Noir Art

Where's Nemo? vs. A Whale of a Tale

Taglines were: "The mightiest motion picture of them all!" "The adventure written a hundred years before its time becomes a motion picture to remember forever!" "Walt Disney's Mighty, Magnificent, Memorable *20,000 Leagues Under the Sea!*"

Ah, yes! The 1954 film, starring James Mason as Captain Nemo and Kirk Douglas as Ned Land. Jules Verne's novel title spelled out "twenty thousand" whereas the film used digits. And the movie poster used a comma between the first and second zeroes, but the film's opening credits reportedly did not.

Alas! I read that somewhere—I don't actually know for certain if it's true. "How can this be possible?" Another query could be "Is your story about Jules Verne's tale or is it about *Finding Nemo*?"

Nemo of the second movie could very well be a reference to Verne's Captain Nemo, but I also read that in Latin and in Greek it means, "no one" or "nobody." You may feel these questions beg for extremely easy answers. In fact, they aren't easy. My story isn't so much about either film, but about a little boy watching (or trying to watch) the Douglas–Mason film.

About fifteen years after the film debuted, my little hometown's movie theater revived the Disney classic. I have watched movies in my hometown in a regular movie house and also at a drive-in. I also know of a third cinema once located in town before the others. I know this because my mother told me so, and it had been built across from her high school. I still live in that town today, after having moved away, but we now have no celluloid dream palace in town or the entire county. To see a movie not on Netflix in our home or on my phone, I must drive thirty minutes either east, west, north or south to Statesville, Lenoir, Wilkesboro, or Hickory.

My mom worked at a dime store when I was a lad, and often I would accompany her on Saturdays. The supposed purposes being not to be left at home alone and to help my mother at her work. The actual reason or reasons included a juicy burger and fries from the diner next door, a cone of black cherry ice cream from the drug store on the corner, and the occasional adventure at the "big screen."

Mom had to certainly give permission, *and money*, for me to do these things. It strikes me while writing this true story, I never adequately thanked either of my parents for any of their gifts—especially their time and love. The greatest parental gifts of all!

On this particular Saturday afternoon, I asked to see this motion picture, at the time, believing a league had something to do with baseball. Who knew? Friends may never suspect, but I was a rather shy child. I felt at home entertaining myself with imaginary adventures in my mind or acting them out like the heroes on the screen, and I loved movies very much.

Sears Theater was one block up the street from the dime store where my mother worked. In plenty of time to see the picture, I walked up the sidewalk, past the burger stand, the black cherry ice cream and comic book drug store, hung a right and crossed the street to the theatre. I suddenly realize how many of these memories are no longer here in town. Only I remain to tell this story.

There was no line of people at the ticket window and no attendant seated there. Pacing up and down the sidewalk outside the magical movie house, I waited for my opportunity and wondered about this nautical story of a decade and a half in movie terms and more than a century by those literary.

Where's Nemo? vs. A Whale of a Tale

Finally, a lady who worked at the cinema looked out the front door at me and asked if I wanted to see the movie. "Yes, ma'am. I do." I paid my dollar for my adventure and skipped the popcorn and drink. Then and only then, the lady said no one else had come to see it, and the movie had already started.

That was odd. Not so much that I was the sole audience member but that they strictly kept the scheduled showing times when there was no audience. In this case, "Now Showing!" actually meant "*Now* showing!"

I walked up the ramp to witness the Nautilus and the giant squid. I was indeed the only person in the theater viewing area, and the nice lady was right. The picture had already begun. Not a problem! I had that handled.

See, when Dad took Mom and me to see a movie, we were never on time. It wasn't like we were late on purpose. It just happened that way every single time. Usually, it was the "Coming Soon" advertisements and the film's first ten minutes we missed. We would sit down, watch what we could of the movie until its ending, remain seated, and then see the opening of the three o'clock show when the five o'clock began. Then, the Kerleys would return home, and I'd mentally place the missing ten minutes in the beginning where they belonged. The movie then made sense. The process made sense, although the second audience must have thought we didn't like the show.

I know what my readers must be thinking. This would never happen because after everyone exits the theater, staff quickly clean up the place and admit the next customers. They don't allow someone to see the picture twice or see it at all without purchasing a ticket. This is correct, of course, but the film industry must've been more trusting back then. Did movie moguls change this? Or was it the Kerley Gang? Some questions are better left unanswered.

So, I sat down to watch *20,000 Leagues Under the Sea*. I could sit in *any* seat I wanted. I could sit in all of them if I chose. And I *did*. When I saw "The End" on the big screen, I knew it really wasn't. It was "the beginning." I sat there in silence. After a bit, I imagined I must be experiencing some technical difficulty, as the wait seemed strangely long.

The same staff worker magically appeared and said I'd have to leave. "Was there a fire?" I wondered. My mom isn't going to like that. Were the throngs of movie-goers so large I would be denied seeing the last part of the movie first and the first part last as was the Kerleys' custom? Oh, my daddy isn't going to stand for this, I thought.

Then the "giant squid" curtly informed me that nobody (in Latin and Greek, that would be "Nemo") had shown up for this showing either and they would not run the projector again. Unthwarted by my timid protest, she ejected her sole patron. So, this is the story of how I didn't see *20,000 Leagues Under the Sea* or all of it, anyway. With my stubborn streak a mile wide, I vowed I never would.

I took a different approach on this story's connection to *It's a Wonderful Life*. I couldn't really think of one except that the Bijou was playing *The Bells of Saint Mary's* on that Christmas Eve. Bing Crosby and Ingrid Bergman were Father O'Malley and the headmistress, Sister Mary. She and the other nuns, unlike the Father, believed the deteriorating school could be saved, possibly in the form of charity from a wealthy business owner—played by one Henry Travers. This film was from 1945. The next year, the same actor played Clarence in *It's a Wonderful Life*. I realized that may be stretching here and consulted my *This Wonderful Life* Director, Josh Scott, to see what he thought.

Josh pointed out that while I felt I was alone in the theater, someone was up top rolling film through the viewer. The ticket taker, although at this time I felt I had been treated unfairly, she most certainly saw to it that I was safe. Mom was only a block away, and I know the lady who scooped up my black cherry ice cream at the drugstore and the man who flipped the burgers at the diner wouldn't let anything bad happen to me. I wasn't really alone. Even if I felt I was alone and going through something big, like George Bailey did on Christmas Eve 1945, our Father in heaven watched over us both.

> "For I know the plans I have for you," says the LORD. "They are plans for good and not for disaster, to give you a future and a hope." (Jeremiah 29:11)

> Therefore, whenever we have the opportunity, we should do good to everyone—especially to those in the family of faith. (Galatians 6:10)

> Two people are better off than one, for they can help each other succeed. If one person falls, the other can reach out and help. But someone who falls alone is in real trouble. (Ecclesiastes 4:9–10)

> "But the time is coming—indeed it's here now—when you will be scattered, each one going his own way, leaving me alone. Yet I am not alone because the Father is with me. I have told you all this so that you may have peace in me. Here on earth you will have many trials and sorrows. But take heart, because I have overcome the world." (John 16:32–33)

> Then Jonah prayed to the LORD his God from inside the fish. He said, "I cried out to the LORD in my great trouble, and he answered me. I called to you from the land of the dead, and LORD, you heard me!" (Jonah 2:1–2)

> Do not be afraid or discouraged, for the LORD will personally go ahead of you. He will be with you; he will neither fail you nor abandon you. (Deuteronomy 31:8)

Cues to Clues to Truths

#15 God will not leave us.

He will not let us face life by ourselves.

Burning Down the Dream House (and Sense of Right and Thong)

This story has two parts. I learned a valuable lesson in each. One soothed and one upset. I will begin with the latter, and recall two lines from the Talking Heads' "Burning Down the House" which is not about arson at all. "Don't want to hurt nobody, Some things sure can sweep me off my feet." ("Talking Heads—Burning Down The House lyrics | Lyrics Freak")

Both parts are about avoiding the sting of poor decisions. In both, my father was my patient teacher. In "Sense of Right and Thong," I learned too late I must have said something insensitive and also knew I had to take responsibility for it. Confused, right? Let me carefully try to explain, for that is what my father did in both instances.

Webster explains a thong can be an article of swimwear or underwear, a sandal, or a strip of leather or hide. I don't recall the first definition really being a thing when I was young. For me being funny *was* a thing, but I learned too late the wrong kind of humor can be hurtful.

I remember vividly asking my dad, "What is a thong?" I don't remember specifics in his reply—only that he took patient pains to teach his inquisitive child—only for him to learn his sassy son set him up for a cruel joke.

After his elaborate lesson which I do not fully remember, I unamusingly exclaimed, "Oh! I thought it *wath thomething Thinatra things*." Fans of Ol' Blue Eyes, forgive this shameful, insensitive child. My father did immediately and that stuns me to this day. His calm reaction that shielded a sense of hurt and anger made me realize some things aren't funny. I wished then, and still do, that I could take it back.

The other lesson has to do with another of my favorite films, *Spencer's Mountain*, with Henry Fonda and Maureen O'Hara. Out of all my best-loved movies, I believe this one is the least talked about. Wasn't it compelling to others?

For me, it has so many emotional scenes—cringing as Clay sings loudly and off key when he finally comes to church, being comfortably lulled by an opinionated handyman and his brilliant housewife raising a large family in Wyoming, laughing aloud at zany shenanigans, nauseating pits in my stomach for his oldest son, Clayboy, realizing his first love and not affording college with her, weeping uncontrollably when the felled tree harms the old man with his son endangering his own life to save his father, exhausted as Clayboy runs for help, choking back more tears as grandmother offers piddling life savings and advice about the stars, and grief turning to joy in the lyrics and melody of "In the Garden."

But just as powerful, although I couldn't reason why it was so or why it had to happen, was when Clay burned down his dream house. I couldn't believe it! My young mind couldn't possibly fathom Mr. Spencer's decision.

I do remember much more of the actual part of this lesson. Daddy was just as patient as all the other times before. He retold the events in his own words, with Clay pouring gasoline over the framework of the unfinished dream house, lighting the match only to memorably watch his dreams turn to smoke, how he returned to his family and immediately began repairing loose cabinet doors on their existing home, and his wife saying ultimately that *this* home was her dream house.

Dad lovingly described why a father might do those things. Every good parent wants a better life for their children. Their hopes are to teach them the secrets to life easily without having them learn the hard way.

He recounted how Clay burned the house and sold his land on the mountain so that Clayboy might go to college. Part of it may have been

Burning Down the Dream House (and Sense of Right and Thong)

a rash judgment or impressionable filmmaking. It seemed such a waste to burn the frame of the house if he was selling the property. My father told me that in addition to sacrificing Mr. Spencer's dream house, he was also providing what he believed in his heart was right for his family. My dad taught me that the Spencers had another dream that was even greater—one that burned within them—the dream of education.

I must've seen it at least a little bit, if he didn't spend money on the house that was in one sense selfish, he could use that money and more money from selling his mountain property to pay for his son's college education. Clayboy would be the first in his family to do so, and he could help pave the way for his brothers and sisters. But I still couldn't see why Mr. Spencer had to burn it. Couldn't he have sold it just like he did his mountain? Couldn't he have at least sold the lumber and not destroyed it?

Again, it was probably movie drama. My dad took the approach that Clay Spencer loved the dream of his dream house. A large, beautiful home, not just a house, for his large, beautiful family, overlooking the beauty God had made on that mountain. The dream deeper in his heart was to do the right thing for his family. The initial dream of a better home gave way to the better dream of a better life. In part, perhaps it was Mr. Spencer's way of doing what was right in the right way for the right reasons. A way that would be impactful, not just on a little boy, but also on any selfish feelings that could crop up later. It also closed a door to the old dream. There was no going back.

I can't recall it all, and I'm certain he did a much better job of explaining than me. Although "In the Garden" is about the presence—the powerful presence—of our heavenly Father, it reminds me of both my fathers.

> And He walks with me
> And He talks with me
> And He tells me I am His own
> And the joy we share as we tarry there

None other has ever known.
He speaks and the sound of His voice
Is so sweet the birds hush their singing
And the melody that He gave to me
Within my heart is ringing.

The part of *It's a Wonderful Life* dealing with Peter Bailey had very little screen time. As a young man, I know I didn't grasp in the slightest what motivated George's father. In my great age and ever so slight wisdom, I've come to see more soundly that Peter did want his son to work at his business, not just for a few years, but to carry on a legacy. Intermingled there and more selfless was Peter's understanding that George had dreams of his own, and father wanted his son to be happy.

For trivia aficionados, Ellen Corby was the customer asking for seventeen dollars and fifty cents during the bank run scene of *It's a Wonderful Life* who later played Grandma Walton on the TV series, *The Waltons*. That show was developed from the movie, *Spencer's Mountain*.

> *Seek the Kingdom of God above all else, and live righteously, and he will give you everything you need.* (Matthew 6:33)

> *Take delight in the LORD, and he will give you your heart's desires.* (Psalm 37:4)

> *Rejoice in our confident hope. Be patient in trouble, and keep on praying.* (Romans 12:12)

> *For I can do everything through Christ, who gives me strength.* (Philippians 4:13)

> *Young people, it's wonderful to be young! Enjoy every minute of it. Do everything you want to do; take it all in.*

Burning Down the Dream House (and Sense of Right and Thong)

But remember that you must give an account to God for everything you do. So refuse to worry, and keep your body healthy. But remember that youth, with a whole life before you, is meaningless. (Ecclesiastes 11:9–10)

Commit your actions to the LORD, and your plans will succeed. (Proverbs 16:3)

Trust in the LORD with all your heart; do not depend on your own understanding. Seek his will in all you do, and he will show you which path to take. (Proverbs 3:5–6)

We can make our plans, but the LORD determines our steps. (Proverbs 16:9)

For God has not given us a spirit of fear and timidity, but of power, love, and self-discipline. (2 Timothy 1:7)

Cues to Clues to Truths

#16 God promises us love and self-control.

The Spirit stirs within us desires to resist sin and also helps us to think soberly and wisely.

Locked Out or Locked Up (That is the Question)

I admit it. This story is about me being a jerk. It was bound to happen, right? I confess this one time, but we both know there have been others.

My friends and I had gone out. I got home at a decent hour with my friends dropping me off. I was tired and ready to go to bed. After they left was when I discovered I didn't have my house key. Mom and Dad were asleep. I was a little annoyed that I was locked out but felt it would be all right. Mom was a light sleeper, and a knock on the door or a ring on the doorbell should do it. I hated to wake her, but I didn't know what else to do. Dad could sleep through a magnitude 9.5 earthquake.

I was glad I couldn't possibly disturb him. I rang the doorbell for Mom, but nothing happened. I rang a few more times. I couldn't understand why Mom wouldn't wake up. I trusted she and Dad were okay, but I needed sleep. I followed that bell ringing with some strong knocks on the door, with no change in the results.

There was a broom handle in the garage, so I started tapping on windows with it. Still nothing. I went around the house and tapped every window I could reach. I worked my way around the house to the front door. I laid into the doorbell there and gave a few good raps on the door.

About that time, a car pulled in the drive. Had my friends returned? They shouldn't have left me with no way to get into my own home in the first place. Randy? Kevin? Randy and Kevin didn't answer because they weren't there. The car in question was a county deputy's patrol vehicle.

"Hello, Officer. May I help you?" In a gruff voice, he said, "A lady called that someone was trying to break in." "Well, Sir, Mom must mean me—because I haven't seen anyone else." He checked out my story with me first, and then radioed to dispatch. Dispatch called Mom to tell her that the burglar was her son.

The kitchen door cracked open ever so slightly, and my poor, terrified Mama peered out. "Why didn't you say it was you?" Well, I did say it was me. I yelled, knocked, rang the doorbell, and tapped on the windows. Mother didn't need to hear all that. I went to sleep quickly, but Mom must've been awake most of the night. I am sorry, Mom. You deserved better.

Oh, yes! That broomstick? When the deputy rolled up, I slung that thing as hard as I could sling it. As far as I know, I think it never came down. It must still be in orbit!

Bert, played by Ward Bond, was the police officer from *It's a Wonderful Life*. He and Ernie the cabbie were good friends of George's. Bert sent them champagne on their wedding day. Later, he taped travel posters over the broken windows at 320 Sycamore for their honeymoon suite, and he and Ernie sang, "I Love You Truly" for the newlyweds. On that Christmas Eve, he came looking for George when he saw George's car had crashed into a tree. In the Pottersville sequence, he was doing his job as the good police officer he was. He just didn't know George for George had never been born. Still, that wasn't enough reason to shoot at him.

> *Surely your goodness and unfailing love will pursue me all the days of my life, and I will live in the house of the LORD forever.* (Psalm 23:6)

> *He is the Rock; his deeds are perfect. Everything he does is just and fair. He is a faithful God who does no wrong; how just and upright he is!* (Deuteronomy 32:4)

> "In the future your children will ask you, 'What is the meaning of these laws, decrees, and regulations that the LORD our God has commanded us to obey?'" (Deuteronomy 6:20)

> Give justice to the poor and the orphan; Uphold the rights of the oppressed and the destitute. Rescue the poor and helpless; deliver them from the grasp of evil people. (Psalm 82:3–4)

> The authorities are God's servants, sent for your good. But if you are doing wrong, of course you should be afraid, for they have the power to punish you. They are God's servants, sent for the very purpose of punishing those who do what is wrong. (Romans 13:4)

> Even when I walk through the darkest valley, I will not be afraid, for you are close beside me. Your rod and your staff protect and comfort me. (Psalm 23:4)

Cues to Clues to Truths

#17 Even in our darkest moments, we can always turn to Him for He is always by our side, and always ready to help.

Our God guides us in troubles and even through correction.

Petals and Wings

It may seem from this title that I am beginning with the *It's a Wonderful Life* portion instead of a true story from my life. My selected title could suggest Zuzu's petals and Clarence's wings. This is correct, but it has a different purpose here. Something noticed, without fully remembering it later or it doesn't seem to resonate at all.

I need to clear that up. Remember George Bailey's prayer at Martini's Bar on Christmas Eve? George, admitting he wasn't a praying man, asked for God's help while in an unlikely place. Surrounded with friends, he felt more alone than he ever had before.

Historians of this great film know that Jimmy Stewart, our George Bailey from Bedford Falls, had recently returned from the Second World War, a pilot who had flown many missions. He was a movie star who did his part unselfishly for our country. Back then, they may have referred to what current soldiers know as PTSD or post-traumatic stress disorder by several other names: combat fatigue, battle fatigue, or shell shock.

I believe when watching that scene, I see a great actor dealing with PTSD. Doing his job as he did during the war, it certainly fits the man. Through further study, I notice that clip to be a bit grainy for Frank Capra had it enlarged to convey the emotion. Some say Mr. Stewart told Capra he couldn't do it again, so he was happy that he completed the scene in that one shot.

But what else was going on in that scene? It was Christmas Eve and patrons were having a drink and celebrating with friends. It was a bar after all, so maybe there was music? Yes, that is right! Adriana

Caselotti was singing, "Vieni, Vieni." In one part of the song omitted from the film:

> Palm trees are gently swaying
> My heart is saying
> How much I love you
> Ah, moonlight is softly gleaming
> My heart is dreaming of you

Those lyrics remind me of George and Mary's love, but the feeling in the music is very different from what George was experiencing. In my reading and research, I learned that Adriana was the voice of Snow White, and in another of my favorite movies, she voices Juliet in *The Wizard of Oz*. "Wherefore art thou, Romeo?"

Other songs from *It's a Wonderful Life* include: "Buffalo Gals," "Twinkle, Twinkle, Little Star," "Charleston," "My Wild Irish Rose," "Avalon," "Wedding March," "The Stars and Stripes Forever," "Song of the Islands," "I Love You Truly", "This is the Army, Mr. Jones," "When Johnny Comes Marching Home," "O Come All Ye Faithful," "Hark the Herald Angels Sing," "King Porter Stomp," "O Sole Mio", and "Auld Lang Syne."

This brings me back to my title. It calls to mind for me two lines near the end of a song in which every line is so beautiful and moving. The song is "It's a Wonderful Life" by Michael B. White. It is a memorable retelling of the Christmas movie classic I love so much.

For our one-person show of the story, *This Wonderful Life* by Steve Murray, I knew we must include the song in our production. Before our first-time presentation to our Producer Caleb Sigmon, Director Josh Scott played Michael B. White's song and I wept at the first few notes.

The first twenty-five seconds would be played for my entrance, and that launched me into seventy-five minutes of Steve Murray's play. At curtain, Michael's song was played in its entirety. Eleven months prior to the engagement that was still a leap of faith, I asked for Michael's permission to use his song in our production. He was so very gracious and kind, saying, "Hearing that it has meant something to you and that you will share it is all a songwriter needs to hear!" I feel the same way with theater. When I updated Michael ten days before our show, he left me with, "May the holidays ahead remind us all, just how fortunate we are to be alive and healthy, especially now!"

If flower petals symbolize fragility, then wings represent not only the ability to fly, but improvement, freedom and spirituality. I share here a portion of Michael B. White's masterpiece, four lines at the end tying together perfectly the two objects in my story title:

I've got Zuzu's petals
And now Clarence can fly
I've got all the proof I need
That it's a wonderful life

It's a Wonderful Life is a 1946 American classic fantasy drama film produced and directed by Frank Capra, based on the short story and booklet *The Greatest Gift* which Philip Van Doren Stern self-published in 1943 and is in turn loosely based on the 1843 Charles Dickens novella *A Christmas Carol*. ("It's a Wonderful Life | Oscars Wiki | Fandom") The movie, *A Christmas Carol* opened in 1951. Both movies mentioned here were considered disappointments when they were released. Having something in common other than Christmas, the two classics owe their success through television.

> *Sing to him; yes, sing his praises. Tell everyone about his wonderful deeds.* (Psalm 105:2)

> *And what do you benefit if you gain the whole world but lose your own soul? Is anything worth more than your soul?* (Matthew 16:26)

To all who mourn in Israel, he will give a crown of beauty for ashes, a joyous blessing instead of mourning, festive praise instead of despair. In their righteousness, they will be like great oaks that the LORD has planted for his own glory. (Isaiah 61:3)

Cues to Clues to Truths

#18 God will comfort all who mourn with beauty, righteousness, gladness, and thanksgiving.

Jesus can transform our condemnation, hopelessness, ungratefulness, and despair into the gift of joy.

"Two Georges" by Greg Clark Noir Art

Best Boss EVER

(Description of textile industry job)

Cloth Doffer—Cloth handler, loom doffer. Removes rolls of cloth from looms and trucks cloth to storage. Pulls lever or presses button to stop machine when roll has sufficient yardage as indicated by yardage clock, mark on cloth, or color-coded card flag. Turns handle to lower roll of cloth, cuts cloth using scissors, and places cloth roll on hand truck. Places empty take-up beam on bracket of machine, attaches cloth to beam, and restarts machine. Writes identifying information, for example lot and style number, on ticket and attaches ticket to cloth roll. Trucks cloth to storage or inspection department. May also weigh and keep record of cloth beams doffed.

I've had several good bosses. My best supervisor, however, was my very first one and from the textile industry. I was hired to be a cloth doffer and trained by Mickey, a friend I had known for several years. He had turned in his notice in order to take another job. I trained for one week with Mickey, and then I was on my own.

It was a very physically demanding position. Mickey and I had both played high school football. Okay, Mickey played varsity ball in high school. I was a blocking dummy for junior varsity practices and warmed the bench during games.

Everyone in our section of the Weave Room was accepting of me and gladly offered help when they could. I realized they had their own jobs to do. I needed to pull my own weight. The workplace was hot, loud, and if you were not extremely careful, dirty. Not only did I have to carry out all the responsibilities listed earlier, but I also had to make sure the cloth remained as clean as possible during the entire process. Imperfections in the cloth were graded in the inspection department, including soiled cloth, not just mistakes that occurred when weaving it. If not careful, I could lessen the grade of a roll of cloth if I were to get it dirty. There was absolutely no time to loaf around.

The time came to receive my first check for my first job. On top of all his other duties, Phil Coker would hand out the paychecks to his team each payday. He gave me my check and left to pay the rest of our team.

I looked at the check and knew I hadn't earned that money. I felt guilty, practically stealing from the company. I went to Mr. Coker and gave my check back. His face was the face of surprise. He was much taller than me, the weave room was extremely loud even with everyone wearing ear protection, and I yelled up to his ear so he might hear me, "I can't do this job! I don't deserve this money!"

He motioned for me to follow him. I figured I was in big trouble but didn't dare stay behind. Mr. Coker led me to the supply room where fixers got the necessary parts to repair their looms. It was the quietest place near our area, and he wanted to know what was wrong. I was almost in tears but explained I couldn't do what Mickey did. My boss said, "Come on. Let's go back out there." I would've rather been just about anywhere else, but again I followed him.

He took me to a loom which was on my list to doff, and I showed him how I struggled. Mickey would squat in front of the roll of cloth that was slowly spinning on the loom, remove it and rest it on his thighs, write the style number and loom number on the roll, cut the cloth and attach that to an empty roller and put it back in place, all the while with that heavy roll of cloth on his legs. Mickey was a strong young man—I was just young. I put that roll of cloth on my cart and headed for another roll to doff. This time, Mr. Coker took the lead. He cut the cloth first, popped the roller out easily, threw the roll of cloth over his shoulder, and carried it to the cart. He then returned and started a new roll. The information was written on the cloth and on a card that would accompany it to the grading room.

I tried his way on the next loom and could manage much better. I had believed that Mickey's way was the only way. I had to learn the hard way that I wasn't strong enough to compete with Mickey and his technique, but I knew I'd continue to improve with my boss's way. It still wasn't easy but much easier than before. He could've let me go on discouraged, berated me, or run me away from there, but he didn't. I guess he saw something in me that was worth working with and gave me a second chance. We all need them, but people often keep that to themselves.

I worked there in the summers through high school and college to help pay for my education. I seldom learned anything in any workplace that was as valuable as that first lesson from the "Best Boss Ever."

Potter had always tried to shut down the Bailey Building and Loan. When he got a little desperate, he offered George a job with a big salary. It was tempting at first, giving him a couple of business trips to New York each year and maybe occasionally to Europe. In seconds, George realized he did not want to work for Mr. Potter. George made the right decision. He would've had to do that job Potter's way, and Potter would probably have fired him the first chance he got. If George left the Building and Loan, it most surely would have gone under. The whole town would have suffered soon after.

> *Slaves, obey your earthly masters in everything you do. Try to please them all the time, not just when they are watching you. Serve them sincerely because of your reverent fear of the Lord. Work willingly at whatever you do, as though you were working for the Lord rather than for people.* (Colossians 3:22–23)

> *Never be lazy, but work hard and serve the Lord enthusiastically. Rejoice in our confident hope. Be patient in trouble, and keep on praying.* (Romans 12:11–12)
>
> *A hard worker has plenty of food, but a person who chases fantasies ends up in poverty. The trustworthy person will get a rich reward, but a person who wants quick riches will get into trouble.* (Proverbs 28:19–20)
>
> *I tell you, you can pray for anything, and if you believe that you've received it, it will be yours.* (Mark 11:24)

Cues to Clues to Truths

#19 God promises to answer our prayers.

He grants His children the desires of their hearts as long as it will do them good in the long run. Abide in Christ, live for Him, be in line with the will of God, have faith in God, and He will move us to pray the prayers we will have faith for and believe we have received it.

The New Jack Pumpkinhead

If you know Jack Pumpkinhead, you must be a fan of Lyman Frank Baum, and not just *The Wonderful Wizard of Oz*. Pumpkinhead is a fictional character from *The Land of Oz* and appears in several of the Oz books.

My first play (if you don't count the first grade Christmas show) was *The Wizard of Oz*. I auditioned for the Cowardly Lion role and was offered the Wizard instead. I always wanted to be in a play but was afraid of failure. It took me a long time to realize that refusing to risk is the ultimate failure. I had always promised myself that if a theater nearby would produce *The Wizard of Oz*, I would finally audition. I wanted to channel Bert Lahr. I often did at home and for a small circle of friends but never for strangers.

The experience was tough, and I waited a year before I went out on that limb again. I was glad I did it, but the next play if there was a next one, had to be the right one. So why was this new experience so difficult for me? There are several reasons, and this story only deals with one of them.

The show was to open in the fall. Think "pumpkins." I was naive back then, thinking the movie I loved so much would be just like the play and vice versa. The gist was similar with several twists that I didn't understand fully. Some twists were in the script, and some were later divulged.

This was the big one. Know the big artificial pumpkins that serve as outdoor Halloween decorations? That was going to be the wizard's head! Buy a big fake pumpkin, paint it green, then paint another face where the jack-o-lantern face once was, attach a hat of sorts underneath, cover my neck and head as if the entire thing was a neck, put it on my head, and voila! I am a pumpkin head!

That was the easy part. The hard part was walking around with that thing on my head. If you have read my story, "Beta Club for Dummies," then you know I insist on doing what is expected of me. On the first night of the show, my pumpkin head fell off! I know, I know. "Don't pay any attention to that man behind the pumpkin head." Very funny.

To say the least, I was devastated. I didn't want to even attempt wearing that huge monstrosity on the show's second night. The guy who got "my" Cowardly Lion role offered advice. He said, "Just put it on and walk around the dressing room for a while." Believe me, I'm not bitter because he truly was the best one to be the lion. He just couldn't see what I was feeling.

"That might help, Mike, if that was all I had to do! But I have to walk in the dark, go through a curtain with virtually a blindfold on, walk up three rickety steps to a platform, pass through an archway that was cut too small and has strips from an old shower curtain hanging from it! Then, I have to do my scene and exit without losing the pumpkin head, falling down, or injuring myself. And they never had that pumpkin head ready for me in rehearsals! Only on opening night!" Yes, I only thought all of that in my head and didn't bother anyone with it. It would've been a good speech though.

Think about Janie and Pete on Christmas Eve 1945. Janie was practicing "Hark! The Herald Angels Sing," and Pete was writing *the* Christmas story. It was all for the party that night and to celebrate Christmas. The *true* meaning of Christmas.

Janie made a couple mistakes, hitting the wrong notes. Pete had trouble spelling "frankincense" and "hallelujah." I mean, who doesn't? They were doing their best, but George was having a horrible night and took it out on them. He was miserable and seemed to want to make everyone else miserable, too.

Everything worked out the way it was supposed to. Even if Janie messed up the fingering of the piano keys or Pete misspelled a few words, and even if eight thousand dollars were missing, George, by the end of the film, was with his wonderful family. I would say that was perfect. And Halloween and pumpkin heads are still ten months away.

> *But you belong to God, my dear children. You have already won a victory over those people, because the Spirit who lives in you is greater than the spirit who lives in the world.* (1 John 4:4)

> *Walk with the wise and become wise; Associate with fools and get in trouble.* (Proverbs 13:20)

> *This is why we work hard and continue to struggle, for our hope is in the living God, who is the Savior of all people and particularly of all believers. Teach these things and insist that everyone learn them.* (1 Timothy 4:10–11)

> *The LORD directs the steps of the godly. He delights in every detail of their lives. Though they stumble, they will never fall, for the LORD holds them up by the hand.* (Psalm 37:23–24)

Cues to Clues to Truths

#20 Our Father promises we will never fall with Him.

In our world of corruption, those who follow Him may suffer and stumble, but it is only temporary. When the ungodly fall, their stumbling will lead to their destruction.

"A Very Bailey Christmas" by Greg Clark Noir Art

All I Want for Christmas (Came on the Fourth of July)

My first two jobs after college were Assistant Manager positions of drug stores. No, not Gower's. Dad called me a glorified stock boy. Basically, he was right.

Wait! I was much more, wasn't I? . . . I did more than stock shelves, right? Yes. I unloaded trucks, built displays and end caps, fronted merchandise, ordered merchandise, dusted merchandise, vacuumed carpet, swept the sidewalk in summer and shoveled snow in winter. I broke down boxes to discard in the dumpster. I climbed ladders to change light bulbs. I counted out registers, did the paperwork at the end of night, and took deposits to the bank. I helped customers find items they were looking for. I stopped what I was doing to ring up a pack of cigarettes. And that was on a slow day.

Okay, all that didn't happen every day. Some days I opened the store. Some days I closed. But we can't forget about the seasons and the holidays every year! Valentine's Day to Saint Patrick's Day to Easter to Mother's Day to Memorial Day to Father's Day to Summer to Fourth of July and back to Summer, to Halloween, Thanksgiving and Christmas. Billy, another assistant manager and a good friend from high school, and I had to see that the merchandise was put out on shelves, displays, endcaps, and aisles. You can't sell goods from an empty cart.

So, this is the problem that people couldn't understand—no matter how many times I tried to explain. Billy and I would be putting out artificial Christmas trees, Christmas wrap, ornaments, candy, gifts, whatever it was for Christmas, and customers would say, "You're putting out Christmas stuff, and it isn't even Thanksgiving yet!" The truth was, it most likely wasn't Halloween either.

We always received our first shipment of artificial Christmas trees during the first week of July. There were varied sizes, and we received several boxes of each type of tree. The trees were in rather large boxes. We knew we would have to assemble one each of the different trees for display, which of course took additional room. All that would fill a large corner of our small stockroom.

Another week and in weeks to come, we were shipped other items. We got Christmas lights, Christmas ornaments, Christmas candy, poinsettias, candles, garland, Christmas giftwrap, wreaths, toys, tree toppers, and I don't know what all. That Christmas wrap alone took another large corner in the ever-shrinking stockroom.

Soon, we had no room left in the stockroom. At times, I felt like we were a warehouse instead of a store. Quickly, we were forced to put out as much of the several types of Christmas merchandise we had accumulated because more was on its way. And then you would hear, "It's not even Halloween yet!" "No, sir, but our Halloween merchandise is just one aisle over," I would often say.

That is when I turned into Ebenezer Scrooge. I didn't like Christmas during that time. I would say I only cared for the true meaning of Christmas, not the commercial part. The truth of the matter was that all of our jobs depended on that commercial part. If I am honest with myself, the true meaning of Christmas in my heart suffered as well. I admit that makes Scrooge look not so bad. Shameful! Just shameful!

Now, I try to do better. I may not hang any decorations, but I try to have the true Christmas spirit all year long.

I believe most people who have seen *It's a Wonderful Life* like it. Many love it. I will say that when we did the one-person play, a substantial portion of the small audience surprisingly had never seen the movie. People have different parts that make them laugh and other scenes in the movie make them cry. Some cry at Clarence's inscription inside *Tom Sawyer*, and others have been crying since George asked Mary if she wanted the moon.

Some people watch it every year at Christmas from start to finish. Many watch at least bits and pieces of it during the holidays. Several see it more than once in November and December, or perhaps even throughout the year.

One may like the love story of George Bailey meeting Mary Hatch. Another person cheers for Bedford Falls' success through George's sacrifices. Another may be drawn to the shocking circumstances that almost pushed him to the brink or thrill when George shines along with the townspeople, and when Clarence gets his wings. George realizing that life really is wonderful has to be one of the top favorites of many fans. Someone may like to study the film and pick out imperfections, not to ridicule but because they are fascinated with everything about it. Lots of people collect mementoes. There must be a few who watch it every year to remind themselves their lives aren't so bad.

Still others may say it was Harry who had the wonderful life—football star, Medal of Honor winner, husband to Ruth Dakin Bailey, and researcher for his father-in-law's company. And still others say life isn't wonderful at all for anyone.

Even if the premise of *It's a Wonderful Life* seems to suggest the contrary, true fans see and believe how much courage, grit, heart, resilience, faith, and hope it takes to decide for yourself that it really is true. If you believe first, you can make it easier for others to do the same.

> *But God showed his great love for us by sending Christ to die for us while we were still sinners.* (Romans 5:8)
>
> *For this is how God loved the world: He gave his one and only Son, so that everyone who believes in him will not perish but have eternal life. God sent his Son into the world not to judge the world, but to save the world through him.* (John 3:16–17)

> *"And you will recognize him by this sign: You will find a baby wrapped snugly in strips of cloth, lying in a manger." Suddenly, the angel was joined by a vast host of others—the armies of heaven—praising God and saying, "Glory to God in highest heaven, and peace on earth to those with whom God is pleased."* (Luke 2:12–14)

> *And God will generously provide all you need. Then you will always have everything you need and plenty left over to share with others.* (2 Corinthians 9:8)

Cues to Clues to Truths

#21 God gives us abundant blessings.

We are blessed by Him so that we can be a blessing to others.

I Really Have a Wonderful (Green Room) Life

A green room is a room in a theater in which actors can relax when not performing. There are a few different ideas how the green room got its name. Green refers to youth. Understudies to major players waited there for their big break. They were inexperienced or "green" actors.

It was where the shrubbery used in plays was kept, and the room became a comfortable place because of the green plants. Or it was because green rooms had almost always been painted green. If the walls and ceiling were indeed painted green, this may have been to ease the actors in composing their thoughts and getting into character. This would be even better if the lighting was kept subdued.

It may have been a custom to shine a red lamp while the show was in progress and a green lamp afterward. Another suggestion might be that since actors may often have to wear stage blood and if it splashed, it would be less noticeable on green walls. Red stage blood on white walls would stand out too much. Possibly, it may be that rooms such as this were lined in green baize to act as soundproofing so actors could run lines.

Still another supposed reason came from old England. A room next to the stage where actors dressed and where the council would meet became known as the "Agreeing room." With an accent it may have sounded like "greeing room" and that sounded like "green room." If performances were held in gardens, maybe actors waited to appear on their cue, under grapevines or trees.

Whatever the true reason is, a green room today may not actually be green. However, the true purpose of green room in the title of this story is for The Green Room Theater at Old Post Office Playhouse in Newton, North Carolina. That is where I had the good fortune to perform Steve Murray's *This Wonderful Life*. A one-man show in which the actor loves the movie, *It's a Wonderful Life* so much, he wants to perform the entire story for the audience.

There was only one performance that Christmas of our show, and that was December 2, 2021. Three very dear friends were instrumental in making it happen—Director Joshua Scott, Producer Caleb Sigmon, and Line Partner Dwight Sherrill. Dwight would drive almost two hours in a single day to help me run lines, learn my lines better, and follow along with the script as I rehearsed the show. He would also keep me on track with my voices and mannerisms for each of my thirty-eight characters. Sometimes even sitting in the cold of our driveway so as not to disturb my wife, who was working from home.

I performed that wonderful night in December after only one rehearsal at the venue. Jonathan and Steve were expert technicians from The Green Room for those two wonderful days in Newton. It was a lot of hard work but definitely the most fun I ever had on stage. Josh says, "If it isn't fun, why do it?" Not everything my friends did for me in preparation could be classified as fun for them in the strictest sense of the word, but they did everything out of love and respect for another individual. Isn't that the lesson that George and Clarence taught us?

There were several friends who came to see my show, some I hadn't seen in a long time. There were many friends who couldn't attend who wished they could've seen me on stage. If it be our Lord's will, we will have another chance at it for He is a God of second chances. Maybe next time I won't forget my lines twice.

Countless times George gave away money he couldn't really spare to almost anybody who was in a jam. His wife Mary sacrificed for her family, for customers of the Bailey Building and Loan, and for the good folks of Bedford Falls. Clarence jumped, not fell, into the river in order to save someone else. Mr. Gower, the pharmacist, bought a suitcase for George in sincere appreciation—a suitcase that must've never left Bedford Falls. Bert the cop and Ernie the cabbie taped travel posters over the windows that George and Mary helped break. On that fateful Christmas Eve, many friends in Bedford Falls gave money to George and Mary. Money that they surely needed, but they wished to help another who had helped them.

> *Whatever is good and perfect is a gift coming down to us from God our Father, who created all the lights in the heavens. He never changes or casts a shifting shadow.* (James 1:17)

> *For all of God's promises have been fulfilled in Christ with a resounding "Yes!" And through Christ, our "Amen" (which means "Yes") ascends to God for his glory.* (2 Corinthians 1:20)

Cues to Clues to Truths

#22 God will fulfill all His promises.

All of God's Old Testament promises are fulfilled in Jesus. God will keep every covenant.

Backstage Mama

"In the performing arts, a stage mother is the mother of a child actor." ("Stage mother—Alchetron, The Free Social Encyclopedia") A stage mom or a stage dad can be a parent or a guardian who aggressively manages their career, usually in what most consider a self-serving manner.

My mother wasn't like that. She saw every show I did, acting or directing. Some she saw twice or more. She passed away on Thanksgiving Day, 2017. I believe she still sees my shows, I just can't hear her cackle or give her a hug after the curtain.

She loved musicals the best. She loved comedies almost as much. Mom didn't get into the dramas very well, but if I had something to do with one then she was there. I took her to as many other shows as I could. Barter Theater in Abingdon was her favorite theater, and her favorite performer there was Mary Lucy Bivins. There are two stages at Barter, and one Christmas I took Mom to see a couple shows. One day, we saw Mary Lucy in *Jacob Marley's Christmas Carol*. The next day Ms. Bivins was in the audience of the other production we came to see across the street. When in the lobby, I said, "Mom, there is your friend."

My sweet mama went up to Mary Lucy and asked, "Did I see you in a play yesterday?" "Yes, you did!" replied Mom's favorite. Anyone would think they had been dear friends for many years—and I believe they certainly were. Mary Lucy is so kind and gracious, and she thrilled my mother.

Mom loved to see shows locally, too. We went to several theaters in Hudson, Hickory, Newton, and Valdese. Everyone loved Mama. If you are reading this and you were in a play my mother saw, she loved every minute of it. If you happened to meet and speak with her afterward, then know you absolutely delighted that lady.

When I heard her laugh from the audience, I knew it was her. Even backstage, among all the other laughter, she could still be heard. Sometimes she found something funny that no one else did necessarily, and she would let loose with a jolly cackle. That would usually start everyone around her laughing—not at her, but her laughter made everyone happy.

She was my support, my Backstage Mama, but in a great way. She was proud of me, no matter what. Even if I went up on a line or missed a cue, she didn't criticize.

There are many specific stories, but I'll tell this one that shows how devoted she truly was. Out of the six shows she had picked which she may want to see that particular production, I took her to the theater with me early as Mama didn't drive. I took her in through the back entrance, walked past the dressing rooms and took her to the steps leading down to the seating. I went back to the dressing room and soon the show opened.

I don't remember which play it was, but I do remember the curtain call and a few minutes afterward. Fans came to see their relatives or children and friends. Mom came up to me and her eyes were black and lower face scraped.

"Mom! What happened?" As soon as I had left her to change, she tripped and fell down the steps. Apparently, her face hit the carpet, smashing her glasses against her nose. My poor mother made everyone around promise they wouldn't tell me until after the show. She didn't want to go to the Emergency Room. She had to see her baby in a play, and she didn't want me to worry.

I felt terrible, but that is only one of the many instances where she quietly supported me so that I could enjoy a hobby or do what I wanted to do. I wish that accident had never happened. I'm so very thankful she didn't break a bone. My mother was tough! Much more so than me.

After that, I made sure she was seated safely before I left her and asked someone to watch over her while I was gone—like she'd always watched over and cared for me.

I believe Mary Hatch Bailey in *It's a Wonderful Life* was the kind of wife and mother that Nell Kerley was. Mary adored Bedford Falls and missed her family when she went to college. It appears she always genuinely cared for George Bailey. She probably could've married Sam Wainwright and lived a wealthy life. She took care of her Bailey family on a modest budget and showed them all how much she loved them. Just like my mom. Mary in *It's a Wonderful Life*, Mary in the Bible, and my mother—Love your children the way they did.

> *"Don't be afraid, Mary," the angel told her, "for you have found favor with God!"* (Luke 1:30)

> *And you must commit yourselves wholeheartedly to these commands that I am giving you today. Repeat them again and again to your children. Talk about them when you are at home and when you are on the road, when you are going to bed and when you are getting up.* (Deuteronomy 6:6–7)

> *Her children stand and bless her. Her husband praises her: "There are many virtuous and capable women in the world, but you surpass them all!" Charm is deceptive and beauty does not last; but a woman who fears the LORD will be greatly praised. Reward her for all she has done. Let her deeds publicly declare her praise.* (Proverbs 31:28–31)

> *And we have a priceless inheritance—an inheritance that is kept in heaven for you, pure and undefiled, beyond the reach of change and decay.* (1 Peter 1:4)

Cues to Clues to Truths

#23 Our Father promises us an inheritance in heaven.

As heirs of God's endless fortunes, that inheritance is not corrupted or short-lived like the world's riches.

"Wishing He'd Never Been Born" by Greg Clark Noir Art

Messenger from a Higher Power

I worked for over a year on a one-person show of the story of George and Mary Bailey, written by Steve Murray, *This Wonderful Life*. The only people who saw any of my early preparation were Josh Scott and Dwight Sherrill. Most of my preparation was usually all alone. So, when I had either of them available or willing to help me, I needed to take every advantage of the time we had together.

It became crunch time, and I realized that seventy-five minutes of material for a sixty-two-year-old hack actor was a bit ambitious. Sometimes while running lines by myself and simultaneously walking laps in the driveway, I would go up on my lines, simply forgetting what I had just recited and having no earthly idea what I was supposed to say next. It might have been the neighbor's dog barking or the blowing horn of a passerby saying, "Hello!" Or it could be a package delivery that broke my concentration.

If working with Josh or Dwight, it was especially important to ignore those distractions, deal with them quickly if necessary, stay in character, and remain on track. When it worked well, I would be performing my one-person show for my one-person audience, see the delivery truck pull into the drive, wait for the driver's approach while still delivering my lines, accept the package, thank them and wish them safe travels, set the delivery down, return to my set, and pick up exactly where I left off in mere seconds.

On one day, I was seated in a rolling office chair that served as Potter's wheelchair, changing from Potter to George and back again, telling the *It's a Wonderful Life* story to Dwight who had heard it all before, several times. Peripherally, I observed an unknown white pickup pull into the drive. I learned later that Dwight hadn't noticed. He was paying attention to his favorite actor.

Uncustomarily, I stopped what I was doing. I didn't stay in character. I didn't know where I was in the play. I was concentrating on a stranger, slowly and tentatively walking toward us, carrying some sort of object. The man appeared to have a slight limp or an artificial leg.

He handed me a small white cross with a note card stapled to it. He emphatically asked me to place it in my yard for others to see it. I remember wondering to myself, "Yep. He's about to ask me for a donation." I don't think I hinted, but he said it was a gift to me, and that I had to agree to give it a prominent residence in the front lawn. He politely hammered that point more than once.

He went on to explain his mission. The cross, and the card especially, were designed to reach out to others and give them hope. If people drove by and saw the cross, they could reflect on what that meant. To me, it means that my savior died on a cross for my sins and for the sins of many—a sinless savior who sacrificed his life as his Father wished. The card, meant mostly for the recipient, was about our country.

He told me our country is hurting now but it is still the greatest country in the world. Thinking instead of a panhandler, now he must surely be a politician, or at least someone wishing to talk politics. Not me, I have always inferred from its name what that is about. The root word, *poly* which means "many" and *ticks* which are blood sucking varmints. Strike two! Wrong again, David.

He shared some more but was interested in what we were doing sitting there outside my garage. Well, brothers and sisters, performing the play was not a part of me at that moment, but I happily explained all about the play, its premise, its origin from my perspective, everything. He, of course, had heard of the movie. I think theater was a foreign idea to him, but he quickly saw the attraction for me. He also swiftly suggested the great need to get the word out. I agree. Much like his "cross of my savior" and his "card for my country." Get the word out!

Messenger from a Higher Power

That wasn't the end of it. I began to pour out my heart to this stranger. But not a real stranger for he instantly became my friend. At the time, I didn't know his name or his history. All my history came spilling out, my failures especially. That was the only time he interrupted me, saying, "That is negative talk. Don't do that to yourself." My new friend was talking to my old friend and me, showing us the truth. In theater, I have learned to be in the moment and to speak the truth. To tell the story. To reach others with the story. To make a difference.

This meeting went on for some time. The old gentleman got up to leave finally, and I asked him his name. He told me, "I'm Bill." After our lengthy conversation, I finally told him my name and introduced him to Dwight. Then, he prayed for us.

After he left, I saw tears in Dwight's eyes. I already knew my eyes and face had been wet for quite some time. I asked Dwight, "He was sent from God, wasn't he?" "Yes, I believe so, David." All the things that had been holding me back, all my mistakes and regrets were in my mind still but didn't sting so badly if I kept what Bill had reminded me in my heart. Dwight had recently experienced a medical ordeal and although he didn't have all the answers yet, he felt a real sense that God was with us. Yes, we knew that before, but Bill certainly got our attention and reminded us.

Trying to get back to the play then, I knew I had to talk to God and thank Him and praise Him first. Later, Denise, my dear wife, asked me, "What were you yelling at?" I wasn't yelling really but shouting, shouting my praises to the One upstairs who loves us, no matter what happens. Shouting and crying and slobbering with my nose running, too! I was a mess, but a much happier mess, and one who was grateful to be reminded of an important message and to be encouraged.

Sometimes God must knock out the bottom boards of our existence to get our attention, but if we have at least a single mustard seed amount of faith in an almighty God, that my friends is how you move a mountain of need in your life! My friend, Nikita Koloff told me, "You can make excuses, or you can make progress, but you can't do both at the same time."

You probably already guessed the link here—Clarence Oddbody! I'm not saying that Bill, who I later learned was a Purple Heart Veteran of the Vietnam War, was an angel. And that part about Clarence failing (there is more negative thinking that Bill warned me about) for hundreds of years to earn his wings and also about a ringing bell signaling the wings had been won really doesn't fit into any doctrine I know. But I do know that Clarence wanted to do everything he could to help George, guardian angel or not. In addition, I believe Bill was a messenger that day.

I knew George helped Harry, Mr. Gower, Ernie, Bert, and countless others, as did Mary. I also believe all those people did what they could to help, not just donating money to George Bailey that they couldn't really spare, but helping everyone in need along the way. Bill helped me, whether he realized it or not. I know it's just a movie, but I think that is a wonderful way to sleep well at night, knowing you helped someone just as God helped each of us. Bill followed His example.

> *May the LORD bless you and protect you. May the LORD smile on you and be gracious to you. May the LORD show you his favor and give you his peace.* (Numbers 6:24–26)

> *"You don't have enough faith," Jesus told them. "I tell you the truth, if you had faith even as small as a mustard seed, you could say to this mountain, 'Move from here to there,' and it would move. Nothing would be impossible."* (Matthew 17:20)

> *Don't forget to show hospitality to strangers, for some who have done this have entertained angels without realizing it!* (Hebrews 13:2)

For the LORD your God is living among you. He is a mighty savior. He will take delight in you with gladness. With his love, he will calm all your fears. He will rejoice over you with joyful songs. (Zephaniah 3:17)

For all who are led by the Spirit of God are children of God. (Romans 8:14)

Cues to Clues to Truths

#24 We are promised guidance from the Holy Spirit.

The Spirit leads every Christian in a specific direction away from their sinful choices and gives us the power to go that way.

Elliot's Synonym of Homonym

Today, I had lunch for the second day in a row at one of my favorite diners. Paying at the register, I saw our local weekly newspaper that I hadn't noticed the day before. On the front page was the photo of a young man I knew over thirty years ago. He is the youngest Black pastor in the county and head chef at a hospital, and only forty years old. His wife, Joyce, owns her own business. I have inspected a few mobile food units in my day, several as a county health inspector and some as a customer, but I bet not many as fine as hers.

Many years ago, when my sons were in elementary school, I volunteered there. I remember working most often with a nice young man named Elliot. His father, Ernest, played varsity football when I played junior varsity. Ernest and Elliot were so good at football, they could play any position. I played bench.

One day, I came to volunteer and said, "What are we working on today, Elliot?" "Homophones, Mr. Kerley." "Excuse me? Let me see your book for a minute." I looked over the pages and discovered that what his textbook referred to as homophones were what I had learned to be homonyms. A homonym is each of two or more words having the same pronunciation but different meanings, such as "n-e-w" and "k-n-e-w." A synonym is a word that means exactly or nearly the same as another word. So, his homophone must be a synonym of my homonym!

While I was figuring this out, Elliot looked up at me and politely asked, "Mr. Kerley, you mean to tell me you're almost thirty years old, and you don't know what a homophone is?" That was over thirty years ago, and it all came rushing back, and today I discovered he is a head chef and a pastor: two incredible achievements, and only one would be outstanding at such a young age.

As an explanation, I prepared a poem or a few lines of prose with homophones sprinkled inside. (Forgive me, parts may be a tad elementary, but that is where I did my best work.)

The sole purpose of this was to have your soul blessed,
Wholly involved in sharing holy wisdom.
Thinking evil or that which is not allowed is just as bad as saying it aloud.
Aye! I did not always know if I had my eye on this.
Many days I was in a daze.
Put the brake on your thoughts to break a commandment.
There is no ceiling to the benefits of sealing in and protecting their hearts.
I should train my gait in the right path if I expect to reach heaven's gate.
If we believe in Him, we are an heir to our heavenly Father in the air.
You cannot buy your way into heaven, or just try to get by. If you think that, you might as well say "bye" now.
Will we see a band of angels if we keep doing what we were banned from doing?
Are you having a duel with yourself on right and wrong? Do you have a dual plan to do good most of the time and what you want to do when it benefits you most?
Whether my point is clear as black and white or slightly grayed, do not feel the need to grade my poem.
Do we put our cares in a false idol? Do we remain idle? Or by taking Elliot's lead, do we alter our lives, trading the back pew for the altar call?
On a side note: To explain in less than a minute what a homograph is, I only have a small or minute chance. Wait! I think I just did.
But know this . . . Of all the many things we pray for—and God answers all prayers—answers that may not be what we want to hear, but

here is the truth. He deserves our praise for everything one prays and especially for answering the prayers we didn't even know we prayed. You see, that sweet young man who taught me about homophones is now teaching the world about Jesus!

Just hold that thought. Teaching the world about Jesus!

It's a Wonderful Life Homophones:

George is most fortunate that Clarence was sent to find and save him. Potter is lucky he didn't get jailed or fined.

Potter believed he belonged to a privileged caste. George should have cast his burdens before Jesus because He cares for all of us.

George felt bored growing up in Bedford Falls. Potter didn't want George on the board of the Building and Loan.

Potter's coarse speech and behavior was rude. George was on the right course for the wrong reasons.

> *Do to others as you would like them to do to you.* (Luke 6:31)

> *Do to others whatever you would like them to do to you. This is the essence of all that is taught in the law and the prophets.* (Matthew 7:12)

> *A second is equally important: "Love your neighbor as yourself." The entire law and all the demands of the prophets are based on these two commandments.* (Matthew 22:39–40)

> *The second is equally important: "Love your neighbor as yourself." No other commandment is greater than these.* (Mark 12:31)

> *Owe nothing to anyone—except for your obligation to love one another. If you love your neighbor, you will fulfill the requirements of God's law. For the commandments say, "You must not commit adultery. You must not murder. You must not steal. You must not covet." These—and other such commandments—are summed up in this one commandment: "Love your neighbor as yourself."* (Romans 13:8–9)

> *For the whole law can be summed up in this one command: "Love your neighbor as yourself."* (Galatians 5:14)

> *Live wisely among those who are not believers, and make the most of every opportunity. Let your conversation be gracious and attractive so that you will have the right response for everyone.* (Colossians 4:5–6)

> *Honor and majesty surround him; strength and joy fill his dwelling.* (1 Chronicles 16:27)

Cues to Clues to Truths

#25 God can provide great glory and joy.

True joy isn't dependent on our circumstances, but relies upon living in faith, light, and purpose.

Another Thing To Be Thankful For

Mama was sick again. Extremely sick. She had been in poor health almost from the day Daddy died. We had thought her health was good, when she had retired several years before to care for him. After his passing in 2000, her health began to deteriorate. By 2016, she was much worse. Early 2017, she had pneumonia. She spent almost two weeks in the hospital and then was transferred to a rehab facility where she got stronger. Coming home, she had a few good months but began to deteriorate again. She felt weak, couldn't eat well, couldn't sleep, and grew more and more miserable. We took her to doctors multiple times, had several tests, but they couldn't determine what was wrong.

This particular Saturday night in November 2017, she couldn't get comfortable enough to sleep. She left her bed and moved to the sofa in the living room. I was doing paperwork in the next room. All of a sudden, I heard my mother say, "There's an angel!" I froze. I don't doubt one bit she saw an angel. I must have been too afraid to go in there, but I listened, and she seemed to calm and doze off. I trust if I was supposed to go to her, I would have. I also trust I was where I was supposed to be.

She transferred back to her bed during the early morning. Later, she called Denise and me into her bedroom. My mama looked at me to say happily, "I'm going home today! I'm going to see your daddy, your son, Michael, and my mama and daddy."

I didn't quite know what to think. Although most people seem to live as though their days aren't numbered, the three of us knew we wouldn't be the ones who determined the end of our lives. Psalm 90:12 says, *"Teach us to realize the brevity of life, so that we may grow in wisdom.*" Mom, Denise, and I knew our time to leave this earth would be when the Lord calls each of us home.

We don't necessarily get a heads-up on the exact day or time, but I wanted to know in that moment what do we do right now? We decided to call for an ambulance, and they took her to Catawba Memorial Hospital. It was determined she had pneumonia for the second time in less than a year and she was admitted. Things were a little better Monday. She responded to treatment. Then on Tuesday, my wife and I both got calls at work to come to the hospital quickly. That couldn't be good. Just like with the peaks and valleys of my son's illness, I thought, "Here we go again."

At the hospital, the physicians explained that although she did have pneumonia, other tests indicated she most likely had cancer. So that explained her pain, weight loss, and other symptoms. Further tests could determine that definitely but was it necessary to put her through that? After discussion with doctors and prayer with the Great Physician, we decided to stop the pneumonia treatments and move her to the oncology unit to make her more comfortable.

Things at that point moved rather quickly. We got word to relatives to come see her one last time. Denise played gospel music on her phone to soothe Mom. We talked to her peacefully, told her she was going to feel better soon and that we would be okay. We would miss her dearly, but we would know she was in a better place. I held Mother's hand and was basically thinking out loud, "Mama, I wish you could tell me what heaven is like." She had been quiet for some time, then quickly looked up and said, "I haven't been there yet."

You would have to understand my mom's unique sense of humor and understanding, but in some way, that was comforting to me. We can imagine what the streets of heaven are like, but we will not truly know until we see for ourselves. That was the last thing she said to anyone. Her last word, *yet,* declares she knew where she was going. I had no doubts either.

Another Thing To Be Thankful For

Remember, she had told us Sunday she was going home. Tuesday was two days later. Was this the day? She seemed to be holding on for something. I believe it was to see one relative one last time before crossing over. She was still with us Wednesday. My wonderful wife and I stayed with Mom that week, but Denise didn't leave. She would encourage me to go home, shower and rest a few hours before coming back. Dee stayed by my mother's side.

Then, it dawned on me that the next day was Thanksgiving. I can often be pessimistic, and at that moment I couldn't bear thoughts of her dying on Thanksgiving Day. I certainly didn't want her to suffer anymore. Jan, a wonderful friend to Mother and our family, offered to stay with her while we went to visit Denise's mother for the Thanksgiving meal.

I've always said my wife is much smarter than I am. It is true. I know it. Sometime the previous day or two, Denise realized that Mom was waiting for, not only that relative, but for the 23rd of the month. When she told me that, I knew she was right. It is the way Mom would have planned it if she could.

You see, there were already some significant 23rd dates in our little family of three. We married on February 23, Denise's birthday is June 23, and Mom's birthday is December 23. For four years, I had joked that if it was the 23rd of any month I need to pay attention because it might be something especially important to remember. Thanksgiving that year was November 23—one month until her 84th birthday.

We drove back to the hospital, Denise let me out to return to Mom and Jan while she went to check on someone's dogs while they were away. Jan was in good spirits, having enjoyed being with my mother. Jan loved her very much, and Mom certainly loved Jan. Dee had to run an errand, and I was alone with Mother. It was a little more than an hour until midnight, another day. Before Dee returned, Papa called my mama home.

She was only four days off from her earlier prediction. Denise was right in saying that Mom was waiting for the 23rd. Mom must have known that if she waited for another relative much more, then it would be the 24th on Friday. After a troubling week of ups and downs, going to her heavenly home on Thanksgiving was the perfect, most ideal way—not something that would be dreadful or horrible.

Mom was home. She wasn't suffering anymore. She was with loved ones, all of them who had gone on before her, some who had been waiting for many years. We will see her again when our day comes. Yes, my mama went to heaven on Thanksgiving Day 2017.

It was another wonderful thing for which to be thankful.

In *It's a Life Wonderful*, a lot happens on the night of Harry's school dance. George has a man-to-man talk with his Pop. He changes his mind and goes to his old high school, to the dance. He meets some old friends there, too—Sam and Marty. He also becomes reacquainted with Marty's sister, Mary. They talk and dance together. They even win the Charleston contest and take a little swim in the pool underneath the dance floor.

George borrows a football uniform for him and a robe for young Mary to walk home in. They sing "Buffalo Gals," and George offers to lasso the moon for Mary. They could not have planned it any better if they had tried. Hiding in the hydrangea bushes after George accidentally stepped on her bathrobe belt and the robe fell to the sidewalk, George was called away from Mary because his father had a stroke. A fatal one.

> *God blesses those who are poor and realize their need for him, for the Kingdom of Heaven is theirs.* (Matthew 5:3)
>
> *My health may fail, and my spirit may grow weak, but God remains the strength of my heart; he is mine forever.* (Psalm 73:26)
>
> *Jesus told her, "I am the resurrection and the life. Anyone who believes in me will live, even after dying. Everyone*

who lives in me and believes in me will never ever die. Do you believe this, Martha?" (John 11:25–26)

For our present troubles are small and won't last very long. Yet they produce for us a glory that vastly outweighs them and will last forever! So we don't look at the troubles we can see now; rather, we fix our gaze on things that cannot be seen. For the things we see now will soon be gone, but the things we cannot see will last forever. (2 Corinthians 4:17–18)

For I know the plans I have for you," says the LORD. "They are plans for good and not for disaster, to give you a future and a hope." (Jeremiah 29:11)

Cues to Clues to Truths

#26 Our Creator provides a secure future for us.

In our times of despair, we must remember that God has a plan for His people, and we can be sure it is filled with a blessing. Realizing our spiritual growth is an important part of God's will for us gives us hope for the future.

How I Didn't Meet Andie MacDowell

I was on the board of Foothills Performing Arts and had read a play I wanted to pitch, *Flaming Idiots* by Tom Rooney. Temple Theater in Sanford, North Carolina, was performing this show, and I decided to get up a band of brothers to check it out. It was October 2010.

In Phase One of my plan, Stephen Starnes, Dwight Sherrill, and I gathered at my mother's home in Taylorsville, North Carolina. Phase Two was to collect Caleb Sigmon at the University of North Carolina School of the Arts in Winston-Salem. The next step of Operation Flaming Idiots was to trek to Sanford.

Stop laughing. It was called Operation Flaming Idiots because of the play, and definitely not us. Not because of Stephen. If you know Stephen, then you know why I must defend him.

The entire trip was about two hours with the UNCSA stop in the middle. Dwight and Stephen stayed with the non-Humvee (That is non-High Mobility Multi-purpose Wheeled Vehicle.) My mission was to check out young Caleb from his dorm.

At the entrance to the building, I would ask for Caleb, and he would come down to join us. Phase Two protocol complete, we made our way to the double doors I had previously entered. As we were about to exit, a mother and her young adult daughter were about to enter. Forever gentlemen, we held the doors open for the ladies. With respect, I cast my eyes downward. When they approached the check-in station, Caleb and I made our way outside. Keep in mind these doors locked for security reasons.

Just as the doors locked behind us, Caleb asked, "Did you recognize her?" "Who?" "The mother," he said. "She's in some commercial." I started racking my brain immediately of my recent television advertisements and it came to me in two phases. First was L'Oreal. Second was Andie MacDowell. Andie MacDowell! *The* Andie MacDowell. The Andie MacDowell from *St. Elmo's Fire, Groundhog Day, Shortcuts, Michael, Multiplicity, Four Weddings and a Funeral,* and others. That Andie MacDowell!

"Caleb! You mean to tell me that she is Andie MacDowell?" I cannot remember his response exactly, just that it was an "Affirmative" and that Operation Flaming Idiots was in action or out of action, depending on how you looked at it. I can't believe how stupid I was to blow a chance like that. I thought about that the rest of the way to Sanford.

We all enjoyed the play very much. Such a funny farce! We laughed and laughed. Stephen's shoe got sprayed with shaving cream or something that accidentally jettisoned from the stage during the show. We had front row tickets. Stephen's shoe and the look on his face were worth every penny of our admission. We laughed back to UNCSA to drop off Caleb at the Andie MacDowell non-rendezvous point, then the older chaps were heading home. In Statesville, we stopped at McDonald's for Mc-MREs, and that was where Stephen's greatest memory of the night took place. It was almost Halloween and decorations were all about. The line to order from the drive-through was quite long and extremely slow. . .

While drafting this story, my mind wandered back to 1981, to a fraternity car wash at a local restaurant, where my roommate, Mike Trice, and I went along the drive-through path, but not in the conventional way. We ordered and picked up without our vehicles. Mike would stomp on the hose lying on the pavement that would signal the culinary team inside. They were surprised to see us walk up to the window. Now, back to McDonald's and the squawky box . . .

I always called the intercom ordering system a squawky box because the voices from it sounded to me like Charlie Brown's teacher. My unsophisticated companions had never heard of such a thing. For some reason, I drove around the stationary drive-through traffic jam that was held up by one weary traveler who apparently had never encountered a squawky box before. They did not know they needed to stomp on the hose that rang the bell that alerted the chef to prepare his fast-food tasty morsels. Actually, it was more like slow-food tasty morsels.

It was not the grub from Ronald McDonald's mess hall, but with all that laughing I had done for over six hours, my gut was screaming. I hurt for several days from my muscle spasming funny bone. I might as well have done a thousand sit-ups.

Caleb, Dwight, Stephen, and David had a memorable evening at the theater. Lots of funny memories! But the most sobering memory for me was how I never met Andie. Andie who my future wife would refer to as my girlfriend. Oh! She is funny, that one! And Dee would reply, "Looks aren't everything." My bride, and the love of my life.

Two connections stand out to me from *It's a Wonderful Life* for this story. Clarence and Mary. With all that Mary and the townspeople of Bedford Falls did for George, it would have been in vain or at least too late if it had not been for Clarence. Mary, over Violet or anyone else, was the right one for George. Her influence was instrumental. In one way of looking at it, George almost let Mary slip away from him more than once.

> *Always be humble and gentle. Be patient with each other, making allowance for each other's faults because of your love. Make every effort to keep yourselves united in the Spirit, binding yourselves together with peace.* (Ephesians 4:2–3)

> *Let no one split apart what God has joined together.* (Mark 10:9)

> *Love is patient and kind. Love is not jealous or boastful or proud or rude. It does not demand its own way. It is not irritable, and it keeps no record of being wronged. It does not rejoice about injustice but rejoices whenever the truth wins out. Love never gives up, never loses faith, is always hopeful, and endures through every circumstance.* (1 Corinthians 13:4–7)

> *And this same God who takes care of me will supply all your needs from his glorious riches, which have been given to us in Christ Jesus.* (Philippians 4:19)

Cues to Clues to Truths

#27 God will meet our needs.

He will provide for our physical, financial, and spiritual needs.

Lightning or Stolen Thunder?

When I was in high school, Dad got this idea we were going to heat the house burning wood. We would install a wood stove in the basement, and we were going to split our own firewood. My father was about forty-five years old at the time, and still more man than I ever was. Our first load of firewood was delivered. Time to get to work! I decided I would not embarrass my father too badly.

It turned out that the work was not as easy as I thought it would be. I don't know if the wood he had ordered was locust, oak, or hickory, but I think it must have been dipped in concrete! Dad had to keep returning to the hardware store to buy new axe handles. We had a fairly good supply of wood to burn just from the axe handles I smashed. The wood was so hard, it was breaking my axe. After the last trip to the hardware store, Dad started calling me "Lightning." "Gee, thanks, Dad!" I remarked with pride. "Is it because I am strong and powerful?" Bursting my bubble, "No, son. It's because you never strike the same place twice." Ouch! That still stings. Dad was wrong about the statement because lightning can strike the same place repeatedly, especially if it is tall or isolated, but he wasn't wrong about me.

Mark Twain was quoted saying, "Thunder is good, thunder is impressive; but it is lightning that does the work." I was the weakest energy spent in the storm against the forest that day. The occupations of all lumberjacks, tree fellers, and wood splitters were safe. Not just that day, but every day before or since, my father was both thunder and lightning. At best, I was only a tiny spark—and that was when my axe skimmed off the metal wedge. I found that made my axe handle last longer.

Let me make this clear. Dad didn't steal my thunder. He didn't rob me of happiness or any good thing. He gave me much more than most people take. He gave me a better perspective. Life isn't a contest. Don't blame someone else for taking something only you can give away. The way you value things comes down to your perspective on what you have—money, belongings, knowledge, whatever. Don't hoard anything you have. Maximize the value of everything you have. The bottom line, I suppose, is this: don't steal someone's thunder, and bring the light without the lightning.

I see the lightning bolt as a symbol of sudden illumination and the destruction of ignorance. If you don't really pay attention when watching the movie, you may not have noticed that snow is falling that Christmas Eve in Bedford Falls, but not in Pottersville. George didn't notice either. He was too wrapped up in his struggle, but there was a glorious time when he realized he was home again. He may be going to jail, but he was going to see his family again.

George's influence may have seemed minor to him, and in many ways, worthless in his eyes. But his neighbors, relatives, and friends didn't think so. I guess Henry Potter didn't think so either, or he wouldn't have tried so hard to ruin him, his business, and family.

> *The LORD will appear above his people; his arrows will fly like lightning! The Sovereign LORD will sound the ram's horn and attack like a whirlwind from the southern desert.* (Zechariah 9:14)

> *Hurl your lightning bolts and scatter your enemies! Shoot your arrows and confuse them!* (Psalm 144:6)

> *The LORD thundered from heaven; the voice of the Most High resounded. He shot arrows and scattered his*

enemies; his lightning flashed, and they were confused. (2 Samuel 22:14–15)

This is my command—be strong and courageous! Do not be afraid or discouraged. For the LORD your God is with you wherever you go. (Joshua 1:9)

Cues to Clues to Truths

#28 Our God will always be with us.

No matter what comes, we can rely on Him. We will never walk alone.

"Please, God, Let Me Live Again" by Greg Clark Noir Art

Who IS This Dude By the Name of Ed Block?

My days of volunteering as an elementary teaching assistant made me incredibly happy. My ex-wife thought that meant I should quit my retail management job and return to college to obtain my teaching certification. So, I did.

Looking back, I was probably more equipped to be an elementary teacher. However, that would have required more than two semesters in order to take other coursework to be more well-rounded. Silver linings, I thought. I had more than enough biology and chemistry credits to teach science at the middle school or high school level. I chose middle school, but that should be its own Kerley Cue story in and of itself. My certificate's reward would be a sentence, I mean span, of nine months.

So approximately eight or ten years after my college education, I am pulled back in. Not unlike Michael Corleone in *The Godfather: Part III,* "Just when I thought I was out, they pulled me back in."

Other students of Lenoir-Rhyne (College then, now University) had been taking courses in their major as well as other general subjects. I was an anomaly—we were in Education Block together, but I was solely and totally immersed in only education courses. Everyone, professors and students, referred to the curriculum in the abbreviated form, Ed. Block.

I don't remember which schoolteacher class we were in at the time, but I can picture everything else as if it happened yesterday. I was in the middle desk of one of the center rows in this unnamed, unknown education class. A young lady, very smart and beautiful but a tad worn down by the chaotic rat race of becoming an educator, looked down at her feet while seated at the desk to my right and screamed in shocking horror flick style, "Look what Ed Block did to me!" The poor tutor-to-be in all her disorder and confusion had on her two feet one brown shoe and one black shoe. We all felt her anguish and defeat. We wanted to help, but didn't know how to respond actually. I can only speak for myself, but I believe we all had a pair of shoes just like hers. Today, we were lucky enough to have left them at home or the dorm room.

It was an eerie trainwreck of a moment when you didn't know if you should look away to save what was left of her dignity or stare blankly toward her like "There but for the grace of God go I." Fortune or misfortune? Fortune or fate? Never forget there is still the blessing of the Divine. Sometimes we miss that.

Driving back home, I thought of my classmate. I reflected on what we all were going through. I had to believe we would still make it. There would be more trials and tribulations. More obstacles and more agony of defeat. Wait a minute, there would also be, if we persevered, what CBS Sports called, "the thrill of victory!" I must answer the call to make sense of it all for her. For all of us!

The more I thought about this story, the more I knew we couldn't give up. The more I thought about her sentence structure, she unknowingly made Ed. Block seem like a person, an evil person perhaps, but still a person. From that thought came this rap I wrote about thirty years ago.

The Ed Block Rap

Now listen up y'all because this is it!
You're gonna hear something that you shouldn't forget.
My name is David Kerley, that's spelled with a 'K' and not with a 'C'
And after we've met, you'll never forget me.
Listen up to what I say

Because I am the Rappin' Special K!
When you talk about student teachers from east to west,
You know the ones from L-R have got to be the best!
But who is this dude by the name of Ed Block?
I hear his name around the clock!
Some people hear his name, and they shake and shudder.
Some people say he is a bad . . . Shut your mouth!
Is he smart, good looking or just a bad dude?
Why doesn't he introduce himself? Isn't that rude?
He may be someone some people don't get,
But how can I like somebody I have never met?
What is his problem? Why doesn't he show?
Who is he to tell me what to do and where to go?
We can throw up our hands and call it quits
or we can stick together and increase our benefits.
I don't mind telling you, this dude really makes me mad.
Let's show this Ed Block who is really bad!

It's a Wonderful Life "Look What Mr. Potter Did to Me"

You have to admit, old man Potter was much more evil than any common, everyday Ed Block. He tried to defeat Peter and Billy Bailey. He tried to defeat George Bailey. He tried to kill the Bailey Building and Loan. But George always stood up to him. As a kid, he defied Potter to talk down to his father, the biggest man in town. At the board meeting after his father's death, George declares, "He died a much richer man than you'll ever be!" When there was a run on the bank, "Aw, you never miss a trick, do you, Potter? Well, you're gonna miss this one." And when Henry Potter tried to become George's employer, "You sit around here and you spin your little webs, and you think the whole world revolves around you and your money. Well, it doesn't, Mr. Potter! In the whole vast configuration of things, I'd say you were nothing but a scurvy little spider."

When it came to Mr. Potter, George didn't feel sorry for himself. He kept his sense of humor about it and remained calm for the most part. He kept on working toward the ideals he believed in. When his back was against the wall, except for a little while on that post-WWII Christmas Eve, he dug in and fought back. He made even more sacrifices so that others wouldn't suffer as he had. Not only was George the richest man in town, I think he was also the biggest. Know, too, that the enemy will stop at nothing to discourage, distract, and destroy.

> *Last of all, as though I had been born at the wrong time, I also saw him. For I am the least of all the apostles. In fact, I'm not even worthy to be called an apostle after the way I persecuted God's church. But whatever I am now, it is all because God poured out his special favor on me—and not without results. For I have worked harder than any of the other apostles; yet it was not I but God who was working through me by his grace.* (1 Corinthians 15:8–10)

> *Stay alert! Watch out for your great enemy, the devil. He prowls around like a roaring lion, looking for someone to devour.* (1 Peter 5:8)

> *For we are not fighting against flesh-and-blood enemies, but against evil rulers and authorities of the unseen world, against mighty powers in this dark world, and against evil spirits in the heavenly places.* (Ephesians 6:12)

> *Fight the good fight for the true faith. Hold tightly to the eternal life to which God has called you, which you have declared so well before many witnesses.* (1 Timothy 6:12)

> *But in that coming day no weapon turned against you will succeed. You will silence every voice raised up to*

accuse you. These benefits are enjoyed by the servants of the LORD; their vindication will come from me. I, the LORD, have spoken! (Isaiah 54:17)

Cues to Clues to Truths

#29 Our Creator will not let us fall to evil works.

God promises His servants who are afflicted and bothered will find protection in Him.

You Must Love Bowling, Huh?

My wife, Denise, and I met technically in rehearsals for *A Christmas Carol* in 2011, at the J. E. Broyhill Civic Center in Lenoir, North Carolina. I'd previously been married. Denise had been engaged before but never married. Through several disappointments apart, we began to believe that we were each going to be alone the rest of our lives. We didn't particularly relish that, but we faced it. We carried on. We had friends in the theater who knew both of us, but we hadn't yet met. This story goes back and forth a little bit to explain how that all gloriously happened, how we met and got married.

Our first date was one week after *A Christmas Carol* closed. We quickly realized in just a few months that God wanted us to be together. We call it "together–together" after a young man we adored who happily learned we were going to see him together in *Christmas Belles* by Jones, Hope, and Wooten and queried for confirmation, "like together . . . together?"

Dates were never really fun for me. It wasn't because of the girl. I felt inadequate. I maybe put too much pressure on myself to enjoy the evening and make a good impression. First dates always seemed to be the worst, and frankly, there weren't many second dates. That first date with Denise was amazing. A great play, a fine dinner, a heartwarming visit with Miller and Macey whom she was dog-sitting for that weekend, and an uncustomary first kiss. Seven years her senior, I still had one hang-up about our date—my age.

"I may be too old," I confessed to her walking into the restaurant. This sweet, young lady gazed into my eyes and reassured me, "You're not old . . . you're ancient." I think right then was when I first thought she may be the one. What can I say, I'm a sucker for sweet talk. Soon we were planning our life "together–together." The names of the two dogs we would have, where we would retire and what we would do when we retired. We also began planning the wedding shortly, but didn't yet share with the world what we were thinking. Since we met at the Civic Center, it seemed a given that the reception if not both wedding and reception should be there.

We did not receive word immediately. Neither of us can remember now exactly what happened but it just didn't work out for that venue. I was somewhat defeated but my bride-to-be had a novel idea for our special marriage venue. She was successful in her first attempt and then had to tell me. Slightly tentative, she was unsure how I would react to the news.

We wanted our wedding to be a celebration and nothing too stuffy. The place she had chosen was none other than Bo's Bodacious Family Entertainment in Lenoir. "Where the fun begins!" as their slogan went. They offered catering, bowling, laser tag, mini golf if not too cold outside, and arcade games. Caleb Sigmon performed a magic show at the reception. A small group was invited for the ceremony. Next, the doors were opened to more friends and family invited to help us celebrate in what many still refer to as the best wedding ever! And not just from our friends' children either.

Some months earlier, introducing Denise to my work family at a fish fry, I let it slip happily that we were getting married in a bowling alley. My coworker's wife, Anita, said soberly and without blinking those immortal words, "You must love bowling, huh?"

George Bailey and Mary Hatch were married in a traditional church ceremony, not a bowling alley, but it was during a downpour! It seemed par for the course, right? George and Mary had had disappointments and they would endure many more, but they didn't let a little cloudburst dampen their joyous special day. My wife taught me that, too. I'm not just thinking about wedding days, but about every day. The wedding day or every day doesn't depend so much on the location, but much more on whether friends, family, and most importantly God, are there as well.

> *Love each other with genuine affection, and take delight in honoring each other. Never be lazy, but work hard and serve the Lord enthusiastically. Rejoice in our confident hope. Be patient in trouble, and keep on praying.* (Romans 12:10–12)

> *Two people are better off than one, for they can help each other succeed. If one person falls, the other can reach out and help. But someone who falls alone is in real trouble.* (Ecclesiastes 4:9–10)

> *Then the LORD God said, "It is not good for the man to be alone. I will make a helper who is just right for him."* (Genesis 2:18)

> *Place me like a seal over your heart, like a seal on your arm. For love is as strong as death, its jealousy as enduring as the grave. Love flashes like fire, the brightest kind of flame. Many waters cannot quench love, nor can rivers drown it. If a man tried to buy love with all his wealth, his offer would be utterly scorned.* (Song of Solomon 8:6–7)

> *Love is patient and kind. Love is not jealous or boastful or proud or rude. It does not demand its own way. It is not irritable, and it keeps no record of being wronged. It does not rejoice about injustice but rejoices whenever the truth wins out. Love never gives up, never loses faith, is always hopeful, and endures through every circumstance. Prophecy and speaking in unknown languages and special*

> *knowledge will become useless. But love will last forever!* (1 Corinthians 13:4–8)
>
> *Take delight in the LORD, and he will give you your heart's desires.* (Psalm 37:4)

Cues to Clues to Truths

#30 God will give us the desires of our hearts.

If our hearts truly find peace, fulfillment, satisfaction, and worth in Him, He will give us what we need.

If a Snake Eats Frequently . . .

Snakes or serpents are mentioned more than eighty times in the Bible. Almost without exception, they are displayed as loathsome creatures who are associated with craftiness and poison. They have become a metaphor for evil in many passages.

In the one year I taught in the school system, I knew a science teacher who raised snakes underneath his kitchen. He also raised rodents in the same room to feed his reptiles. I remember wondering how his wife allowed such a thing. Then, when I later remarried, my wife said we would have a snake one day. We have been married over ten years, and it hasn't happened yet.

You have probably figured out that I've always despised snakes. I do realize some are quite harmless and often feed on pests. On a college field trip, I'd had an encounter with a snake. I think we were at some wildlife preserve in Georgia. This short recounting reveals the only details I remember from the entire trip.

Our tour guide apparently loved snakes of all kinds. She also was determined to get me to pet one of her many treasures within her own den. I mean office. I distinctly told her I didn't wish to hold her snakes, not a single one. Refusing to take "no" as an answer, she plucked up one of her slithering babies and plopped him or her into my hands! I was thrilled.

Yes, I'm being facetious; so was the snake, being facetious. That poor, little thing must have been just as terrified of me as I was of it. I know my hands must have been cold and clammy, and it must have sensed danger. I feel bad for both of us now, but at the time I proved to be quite selfish.

If a snake can poop and I guess it can, this tiny thing gave up an entire Thanksgiving feast in my hands, as I held them over the papers on the snake charmer's desk. Let me just say, she wasn't happy. In my defense, I did try to explain to her in the first place how much I didn't share her love for all of God's creatures. Most of them, yes, but not all.

Maybe I had bought into my mother's fear of snakes and any vermin. Maybe I believed they were inherently evil, but of course they aren't. Since then, I've learned that if a snake eats infrequently, it poops infrequently. On the other hand, if it eats frequently, then . . . well, you get the picture. As a metaphor though, do evil people become more evil as they practice their wrongdoing? I think so, but most evil people do not think they are evil. They probably see themselves as victims or rationalize and justify their hateful deeds.

The way I looked at it, the snake handler was lucky I could hold my bowels better than her offended serpent. Nevertheless, we were both glad when I released the creature to its herpetologist.

I share with you the chorus of a Ray Wylie Hubbard song:

"Snake Farm"

Snake Farm—it just sounds nasty
Snake Farm—well, it pretty much is
Snake Farm—it's a reptile house
Snake Farm—Uuuuggghhh . . .

It's a Wonderful Life — (The Snake of Bedford Falls)

Mr. Potter wasn't the nicest man in Bedford Falls, Pottersville, or any town where he could have resided. On that, I think we can all agree. But how did he end up that way? Was he like Ebenezer Scrooge who had been changed by life circumstances and disappointments? If we were to delve a little deeper here, didn't he have feelings? Or at least at one time, he may have had, right?

There has always been a debate on whether or not people can change. I believe any of us can change, but we have to make a conscious decision to want to do so. Just like beginning to diet or exercise after a lifetime of its deprivation, a new regimen takes time and practice. With age and experience, often there comes a little maturity. Maybe that is what happens to make us desire to change. We realize that what was happening before just wasn't working anymore.

Speaking of change, for we who judge the Mr. Potters of this world, can we change? Can we begin to see possibilities in others for change? If we refuse even the possibility for change, how are we any better than them? I know we must feel we are better to think that, but how can we actually believe we are? It is a temptation to look down on others for whatever reason, but true Christianity doesn't allow that.

> *Dear children, let's not merely say that we love each other; let us show the truth by our actions.* (1 John 3:18)

> *Then the LORD God said to the serpent, "Because you have done this, you are cursed more than all animals, domestic and wild. You will crawl on your belly, groveling in the dust as long as you live. And I will cause hostility between you and the woman, and between your offspring and her offspring. He will strike your head, and you will strike his heel."* (Genesis 3:14–15)

> *O LORD, rescue me from evil people. Protect me from those who are violent, those who plot evil in their hearts and stir up trouble all day long. Their tongues sting like a snake; the venom of a viper drips from their lips.* (Psalm 140:1–3)

See that no one pays back evil for evil, but always try to do good to each other and to all people. Always be joyful. Never stop praying. Be thankful in all circumstances, for this is God's will for you who belong to Christ Jesus. (1 Thessalonians 5:15–18)

Finally, dear brothers and sisters, we ask you to pray for us. Pray that the Lord's message will spread rapidly and be honored wherever it goes, just as when it came to you. Pray, too, that we will be rescued from wicked and evil people, for not everyone is a believer. But the Lord is faithful; he will strengthen you and guard you from the evil one. (2 Thessalonians 3:1–3)

And as we live in God, our love grows more perfect. So we will not be afraid on the day of judgment, but we can face him with confidence because we live like Jesus here in this world. (1 John 4:17)

All who are victorious will be clothed in white. I will never erase their names from the Book of Life, but I will announce before my Father and his angels that they are mine. (Revelation 3:5)

Cues to Clues to Truths

#31 Jesus paid the price for our salvation.

As His people, we will have purity, righteousness, assurance, a heavenly home, and the amazing promise of Jesus confessing our names before the Father.

That's a Pretty Good Story!

After Dad had finished reading a novel or watching a movie, he would say, "That was a good story!" I think he almost always said something like that, maybe sometimes he was more emphatic in praise with his favorites. I don't know yet my father's reaction to my stories but even a mild "That was a pretty good story" for only one of them would mean the world to me. His praise was for fiction. Why can't nonfiction claim the same praise? I think it can, but both forms depend upon the storyteller, don't they?

The Green Mile is the 1996 serial novel by Stephen King. It tells the story of death row supervisor Paul Edgecombe's experiences with the mysterious John Coffey. The Tom Hanks movie by the same name came out in 1999. Although my father died in 2000, I'm sure he never read or saw either. It may be more my cup of tea, but I truly believe Dad would have liked it, too. Especially if he knew what I eventually found out.

I interrupt this story for a moment to tell another on my mom. She often couldn't recall names very well. This is beginning to become a problem with me as I get older. But when Mom was babysitting two brothers or their cousins, two sisters, their names would invariably be, if you listened to Mom, "Buh-Matt and Mah-Ben, Hah-Gretchen, and Gre-Holly."

When it came to recalling actors, she put a unique spin on it. No matter which Morgan Freeman film I was watching, to her he was *Driving Miss Daisy*. If I watched Tom Hanks in *Castaway*, *Sleepless in Seattle*, *A League of Their Own*, *Apollo 13*, or *The Green Mile*, she would ask me, "Is that 'box of chocolates'?" meaning: "Is that Tom Hanks who as Forrest Gump repeated his mother's famous line, 'Life is like a box of chocolates—you never know what you're going to get.'?"

"Yes, Mom, that's him." One time, she asked the same question in a different way, almost getting the name right. "Is that Hank?" "Yes, Mother, that is Tom Hank, singular."

I watched *The Green Mile* after Dad had passed and absolutely loved it. It never ranked as high as Tom's other films. On my first date with the lady I would spend the rest of my life with, I discovered it was also one of her favorites. We each had our own *The Green Mile* story to tell. Hers was, watching the movie when Percy stepped on Mr. Jingles, my bride-to-be stood up in a crowded movie theater and yelled, "No!" Much like the way Stephen King's Annie Wilkes yelled the same thing when Paul Sheldon lit a match to what she believed was the *Misery* manuscript she wanted for her own enjoyment. Denise and Annie were completely different people, but I think you get the idea. I can hear my wife say, "Gee, thanks."

My story I shared with her on that first date about *The Green Mile* was about a trivia (not trivial) connection with the Kerleys. If you have seen the movie, near the end the old Paul Edgecombe, portrayed by Dabbs Greer, is telling about how he was affected by John Coffey. He explains he will live on while Elaine passes, showing the older Paul placing a rose in her casket in the church and later walking past tombstones in the graveyard.

I remember briefly thinking as the "Dabbs Greer" Paul walked among the markers, "STORY" carved on one and "STOREY" on another, "We have Storys in our family!" We do. My father's mother was a Miller before she married and she had relatives whose last names were Story, Storey, and Storie. The cemetery where many of my father's ancestors are buried, including his brother Dillard, is the same graveyard where her Story relatives of various spellings were laid to rest. It is the same cemetery as in *The Green Mile*. In a real sense, I am from that graveyard. I am from photo albums, lockets, mantelpieces, China cabinets, wardrobes, footlockers, shelves, drawers, and storied historic

That's a Pretty Good Story!

hallways displaying and honoring loved ones I never knew and many others I can never forget.

Writing this story, I thought about Harry's stone in Pottersville. Clarence said he died at nine years old, but the marker reads 1911–1919. That would be eight years old at most. Maybe it was a movie mistake of continuity or Clarence's mistake. Think of it this way, Mr. Gower's son, Robert, died around 1919. So many people died between 1918 and 1920 with the Spanish Flu. Think about the lives lost during World War II in the movies but also in real life. If George saved Harry, then Harry didn't die in 1919. In order to save Harry, George risked his own life, and he could've died in 1919.

In another way of thinking, the innocent Harry did fall through the ice and could have drowned. George jumped in to save his brother, but the Lord made it all possible. Their innocence died, but both boys were better for it even though George had a bad ear. If that seems far-fetched and unbelievable, what makes anything about *The Green Mile* more believable? Now, really?

> *There is no greater love than to lay down one's life for one's friends.* (John 15:13)

> *So now I am giving you a new commandment: Love each other. Just as I have loved you, you should love each other.* (John 13:34)

> *But if we confess our sins to him, he is faithful and just to forgive us our sins and to cleanse us from all wickedness.* (1 John 1:9)

> *If you try to hang on to your life, you will lose it. But if you give up your life for my sake, you will save it.* (Luke 9:24)

> *For this is how God loved the world: He gave his one and only Son, so that everyone who believes in him will not perish but have eternal life.* (John 3:16)

Cues to Clues to Truths

#32 God's plan and Jesus's sacrifice provide eternal life.

Anyone who trusts and believes in Him will be saved from sin. We are saved because of God's grace and through faith in Jesus. Life in eternity with God and His Son is the greatest gift. That isn't just a pretty good story. It's the truth!

But I'm Not an Only Child!

People say an only child is spoiled rotten. They say the only child gets everything he or she wants. I know I got more than I deserved, and I know my parents sacrificed to be able to give me more than they had growing up. It all started with love. All gifts in the world but no love would have still been so empty.

Most friends know me as an only child, but I know I'm not. A year or two after I was born, my mother had a miscarriage. Whether the child conceived was a boy or girl, I don't know. For some reason and for many years, I truly believed my sibling was a little brother. Only in the last few years, I have begun to wonder if maybe I was wrong. That perhaps my younger relative was a female.

Regardless of my doubts, I hope they aren't offended by my ignorance. I think what's important is that I love him or her and he or she loves me. I feel that truth. So, in order to help me write this story, I purchased the children's book by Megan Lacourrege, *My Sibling Still*. It is intended for those who've lost a sibling to miscarriage, stillbirth, or infant death. I was struck by the message of love from Lacourrege as well as by the beautiful illustrations of Joshua Wichterich. Both dedicated the book to the little ones they've each lost.

Sixty years later, I was comforted by a child's mind considering why they can't play with their brother or sister but still insistent that love is there. Megan's book did for me what I wanted it to do. I encourage you to get this book if you know someone who has experienced this pain.

What I didn't expect was to be reminded of several other lessons. One of my dearest friends and his wife had two miscarriages before the

Lord blessed them with three other children—not as replacements but as wonderful additions to their family.

The Sunday when my mother told my wife and me that she was going home to see my daddy and my son, I was struck then that she'd also meet for the first time my little brother or sister. This book by Lacourrege reminded me of that beautiful sentiment.

As parents, we weren't the only ones to experience loss when Michael died. His brother, Matthew, mourned for his brother he loved so deeply. I grieve for the loss of Michael but also that as his father I didn't do enough to ease Matthew's pain.

I had tucked away another memory of my Matthew. Matt was a near-miss SIDS baby. His mother's custom when Matt was sleeping as a baby was to let him rest peacefully without noise. For example, if she was folding laundry, she would stack those articles on the living room sofa and not risk waking him if she took them into his room.

For some reason, she didn't this time, and took the folded clothes into his room to place them in his dresser. I believe with all my heart God prompted her to do this for Matt had stopped breathing and was already turning blue but was still alive.

She picked him up and he revived, but what if she had been a minute too late? After taking our child to specialists, we later returned home with a monitor that would detect in seconds if he wasn't breathing. The alarm would sound and then he would start breathing again. It didn't happen often, but when it did, God continued to preserve our precious child. This remained until he was a little older and the monitor was no longer necessary.

Had this not happened the way I have just described to you, Michael would have lost his brother instead of the other way around. I knew all these things to be true but had forgotten how important they were and focused mostly on other things. When I thought of tragedy, I didn't choose to think of all of them at the same time.

Maybe that's another blessing God uses to help us cope. I may think I was too callous to not consider others' loss, but God sees that isn't true.

My baby brother or sister told me so. One day soon, I'll meet them for the first time, and they'll already know everything about me.

And he or she will re-introduce me to their nephew, Michael. I speak to him often still, but on that day and beyond I will know his responses. I will be reunited with my first child and this "only child's" sibling.

I've often thought that maybe my brother or sister should have lived instead of me. That they could've lived a better life, or would've done more with their life; that was me feeling sorry for myself. What I see now is that all of us should live our lives well—not just for us, but for our loved ones who had the same chance at life and have similar regrets, and especially for those who didn't get to live long or at all on this earth and who most assuredly loved us and cared for us, as well as those who cried when we cried and laughed when we laughed. Live for yourself but also live for them. Our lives are made up of two dates and a dash—make the most of that dash.

I have a younger sibling. I am not an only child. I have the best little brother or sister I could ever hope for.

The obvious connection here may be George's little brother, Harry. What if he had drowned when sledding down the snowbank that day? Or what if he had never been born? What about Violet Bick? We don't really learn about her family in the movie. What if Violet had moved away to New York instead of staying in her hometown of Bedford Falls? What about Pete and Janie? Or their younger siblings, Tommy and Zuzu? What if they grew up in separate homes due to divorce or family tragedy? What if they were raised by the widowed Mary? Not every story ends with a perfect ending, but I find solace and hope in knowing God is in control.

> *And we know that God causes everything to work together for the good of those who love God and are called according to his purpose for them. For God knew his people in advance, and he chose them to become like his Son, so that his Son would be the firstborn among many*

brothers and sisters. And having chosen them, he called them to come to him. And having called them, he gave them right standing with himself. And having given them right standing, he gave them his glory. (Romans 8:28–30)

He will wipe every tear from their eyes, and there will be no more death or sorrow or crying or pain. All these things are gone forever." (Revelation 21:4)

This is my command—be strong and courageous! Do not be afraid or discouraged. For the LORD your God is with you wherever you go. (Joshua 1:9)

Cues to Clues to Truths

#33 God will go wherever we are.

God will be with us so that we never have to face battles alone.

"Zuzu's Flower" by Greg Clark Noir Art

A Spoonful of Sugar

The order in which I have authored these stories may not remain when published. Or readers may choose to read them in a different order altogether. I don't think that matters if I can get these stories out of me and the reader can get something out of them. The first story I wrote was "Treehouse Rescue." Many were written in only a day. Sometimes, I finished two or three in one day. However, "But I'm Not an Only Child!" and this one each took a week or longer to write. It was a struggle to get past the title, let alone begin telling this story.

Various titles in my mind referred to "Ninja Parents," "The Last Samurai," or even "Mary Poppins." The story wasn't going to be just one story but points from various stories. Maybe that alone made it more difficult? Maybe the way these stories made me feel uncomfortable made this true?

My intention of this story was to lift up my parents to praise them for doing so much with so little. That is where I first came up with the idea of Ninja Parents, not in the way of my parents being actual ninjas, but in the way of making something out of nothing, having unique skills, and being both mystery and legend at the same time.

Of course, there were practical problems with this. Ninjas were trained as assassins and mercenaries. Watching one of my favorite films, *The Last Samurai*, for the fifth and sixth times recently reminded me Samurai were warriors who usually belonged to noble classes of Japanese society.

I woke in the middle of the night with the thought of a gift that in turn made me think of Mary Poppins. This finally jumpstarted this story that was difficult to begin. Seeing a post from an artist I have been following, Lauren Taylor, brought my intent into perspective for this and the previous story. This post, coupled with one of the songs from Mary Poppins made me think of "A Spoonful of Sugar." I know, this is all quite confusing.

Lauren Taylor suggested your ability to create the reality that you want is directly determined by your willingness to experience the opposite. One example would be working out makes you feel weak when it is actually making you stronger. Digging up trauma will have you feeling broken when it is actually healing you. The story of my unborn sibling and many others fit this idea. This story is about how saving money will have you feeling broke while it is really making you rich. Or maybe it is suggesting all the many ways in which you are already rich. That's where Mary Poppins comes in.

"Treehouse Rescue" came from a true tale of a lean year for my parents. They were moving on from an excellent job in Asheville to a poorer one in Greensboro for less than a year, and then to Taylorsville, my parents' hometown that would later become mine. My story of the treehouse comes from a fun place in my heart although Greensboro was not fondly remembered by Mom and Dad.

In my story about children's death, I gained some healing in various ways I didn't imagine. I gained insight into what life must have been like for my parents from Asheville to Greensboro to Taylorsville, when I was too young at the time to understand. And in that story of my sibling, I mentioned the hurtful thought that only children are spoiled. I'm beginning to see, in a way at least for me, I was spoiled by my parents—not in the way one might think, but truly pampered.

For my birthday that year in Greensboro, I received a Mary Poppins coloring book sans Crayolas. That was literally all, but figuratively I received much more for birthdays and Christmases every year from my parents. I remember a red bicycle with a white banana seat one Christmas, a beautiful loving pup I named Ginger for my twelfth birthday, and various things I know were sacrifices from my parents.

These days, it seems many kids have so much that they don't appreciate anything. At the same time, many children have nothing.

So, in a real way, that coloring book was more special than a hundred bikes and a hundred puppies. The Julie Andrews–Dick Van Dyke classic came out that year, and I think I thought at first and for several years later, it was a story for girls, not boys. Just like I didn't understand all that was going on about me, I didn't understand the film either. Maybe I am just beginning to understand what it means to me.

For me, the movie isn't so much about Mary Poppins. It is Bert that stands out. He may be a one-man band, a sidewalk chalk artist, a kite salesman, or a very chipper chimney sweep, but I see now how he stayed positive through his work. We should do the same. Even if no one tips you for the music you make, or the rain washes away your beautiful creations, or the winds take your best kites to never return except in memories, or if cleaning a chimney or some other dirty job leaves you nothing but tired and dirty. Try to be completely satisfied in what you have accomplished.

That leads me to the song about a spoonful of sugar. It isn't about covering up the bad taste of your medicine. It is about finding fun in everything you do, not just the job. It speaks of the honeybee and robin buzzing and singing while they carry out their otherwise seemingly boring tasks. It speaks of what life would be like if they did not.

I had forgotten that. A little boy whose parents couldn't afford the cost of a coloring book with crayons gave him so much more—things money can't buy. An otherwise unpleasant situation can become pleasant when a pleasing aspect is deliberately introduced. That is the real story of my parents. That is how my father taught me to give even if it hurt and Mom taught me to love unconditionally. They both taught me about Jesus in their own ways.

Some things need to be concealed and certainly others revealed. Many of those to be concealed should be so because of love. Wisdom will allow which approach is needed, through your father and mother. When we get too much too soon, it often proves to not be very helpful.

Potter's wealth and George's riches varied greatly. Henry Potter had everything including owning almost the entire town, but he was unhappy. His belongings did not provide warmth. George felt he was unhappy being unable to afford a new car for his family or carry out his boyhood dreams of travel. Mary and Clarence helped remind him, not just stated by younger brother Harry, that he was indeed the richest man in town.

> *Teach those who are rich in this world not to be proud and not to trust in their money, which is so unreliable. Their trust should be in God, who richly gives us all we need for our enjoyment. Tell them to use their money to do good. They should be rich in good works and generous to those in need, always being ready to share with others. By doing this they will be storing up their treasure as a good foundation for the future so they may experience true life.* (1 Timothy 6:17–19)

> *A gossip goes around telling secrets, so don't hang around with chatterers. If you insult your father or mother, your light will be snuffed out in total darkness. An inheritance obtained too early in life is not a blessing in the end.* (Proverbs 20:19–21)

> *How sweet your words taste to me; they are sweeter than honey.* (Psalm 119:103)

> *Taste and see that the LORD is good. Oh, the joys of those who take refuge in him!* (Psalm 34:8)

> *But all who listen to me will live in peace, untroubled by fear of harm."* (Proverbs 1:33)

Cues to Clues to Truths

#34 God provides for His children a peaceful life.

Those who are wise can rest in the security of the Lord. We needn't fear the eternal disaster waiting for those who ignore God, as we are far more likely to experience joy, peace, and success in this life on earth.

Easy Way to Make a Living

Sitting down and writing, "But I'm Not an Only Child!" and "A Spoonful of Sugar" proved to be difficult. The task was necessary, but I took a little break afterward. When experiencing what I've been told was writer's block, it was hard to get back to writing. My next story on the list was to be called, "A Hard Way to Make a Living." I had always said my job was a hard way to make a living, and it seemed to become harder every year. It did become more difficult, but I see too late my focus on the difficulty made it worse.

As the writer's block went on, I began to wonder if my approach was all wrong. I retired in 2021 from being a health inspector—that person who inspects restaurants and other types of facilities. It is an especially important profession, and I didn't take it lightly. Sometimes I had to tell someone something they didn't want to hear. As human nature proved, if their grade was good, some would nearly break their arms patting themselves on the back. If their grade was low, it was my fault. I realize that seems to be a negative outlook.

Perhaps God wanted me to focus on the good and positive, rather than the negative. If I stayed with "the hard way" in my title and story, there would've been enough material for a book all by itself and that wasn't why I felt God called me to write this series of true stories.

I honestly believe, too late, that had I focused more on the positive during my career, then the work wouldn't have been so draining on me. It would've still been demanding, but maybe I could've handled everything better and not brought the job home with me. I know I could've relied upon the Lord more than I did. In the same way, this changed or evolved story will hopefully be better for me to write and better for others to read. Maybe they can find assurance in their own work and other duties.

There were very good people I met at the establishments I had and with my co-workers in the office. COVID taught me how much I would miss my co-workers when the time to retire actually came, and I selfishly felt a little cheated that for a year, I worked from home and didn't get to see everyone each morning.

We had a good group of people. We were a family. We still are. Retirement didn't change that. Being apart from family sometimes is an unpleasant fact. If you have a conflict with family, work together to deal with it in love and straighten it out. Don't allow hurt feelings to fester. Treat others the way you want to be treated, as we have learned.

I admit we enjoyed teasing each other and that can get out of hand sometimes. I believe if done in a good-natured way and kept in check, it is okay. Stay aware though and if you sense you have hurt someone's feelings, don't make the situation worse. Don't just clam up either. Fix it. I am speaking from experience here, not preaching as if I had no guilt. Don't make the mistakes I made, always have a better attitude, then you will feel better and your work relationships will thrive. Demanding situations will still be meaningful and unavoidable, but that much more manageable with an open mind and caring heart. And with the one who taught us that—Jesus. The easy way to make a good living is to have the right attitude and trust in God.

George never wanted to work at the Building and Loan. In spite of that, he helped a lot of people. He, just like I did, sometimes felt sorry for himself. He felt he missed out on dreams, the promises he had made to himself as a boy. He resented Mr. Potter for his behavior to his father and others, and may have occasionally harbored bad feelings for good friend, Sam Wainwright, who had more money. I think (post-Clarence) George would tell us, "Don't wait to have the floor knocked out from under you before you see what is truly important and wonderful."

Work willingly at whatever you do, as though you were working for the Lord rather than for people. Remember that the Lord will give you an inheritance as your reward, and that the Master you are serving is Christ. (Colossians 3:23–24)

Do everything without complaining and arguing, so that no one can criticize you. Live clean, innocent lives as children of God, shining like bright lights in a world full of crooked and perverse people. (Philippians 2:14–15)

My old self has been crucified with Christ. It is no longer I who live, but Christ lives in me. So I live in this earthly body by trusting in the Son of God, who loved me and gave himself for me. (Galatians 2:20)

Cues to Clues to Truths

#35 God's children experience redemption.

When we follow Jesus, we are cleansed of our sins and have the gift of eternal life. The old version of us is gone and replaced by a new one.

Are You Going to Eat Your Chocolate Cake?

I was bound to have a story on cake sometime. In the dessert line, they asked me, "Would you like white, yellow, or chocolate cake?" I told them, "Yes!"

Dad was diabetic, and I always needed to lose weight. Neither Kerley man needed cake. My father's diabetes was so bad that his blood sugar would drop too low or rise too high with him doing the same activities and eating the same foods as well as the same amounts of the same foods. His doctor believed he was cheating on his diet. I'm not saying he never cheated on his diet, but that was not the sole problem with his condition. The doctor declared he would straighten out Dad's problems by admitting him to the hospital and getting everything regulated. As you have probably guessed, the doctor was mistaken, but what about the cake?

One day, my mother and I went to visit Dad in the hospital. As soon as we got there, we were instructed to go to the administration office. I figured it had something to do with insurance or payments. The administrator looked at us and said, "Your husband (looking at Mom) and your father (looking at me) is stealing our patients' chocolate cake."

My poor mother was so embarrassed. I was furious! What they didn't understand and Mother had forgotten is that Dad liked to tease people. He was funny. Yes, he enjoyed eating anything, not just cake. I could imagine, knowing my father, that he may have said to someone, "Are you going to eat your chocolate cake?" Since longtime friends and even strangers were drawn to my father, I just knew they said, "No, I'm not going to eat it. You can have it." I also know Don Kerley would have then confessed, "Thank you, but I have diabetes. I can't eat your cake. I appreciate you though!" Dad always used to tell me, "Boy, if you are eating something, and it tastes good to you, then spit it out because the doctors don't want you to have it."

Mom was absolutely distraught and had no idea how we were going to look people in the eyes now with her husband a cake thief. I stood up and this is what I said to the administrator, "Unless you see chocolate icing spread from ear to ear on my daddy's face, don't ever accuse him of stealing anything and don't ever mention it to my mother." End of meeting—I never heard anything more about it.

For many years, I would tell this story of how I stood up to defend my parents. Finally, I see I could have handled it much better. I embarrassed Mom worse than the chocolate cake story did. They judged my father unfairly, but I also judged them. Maybe I was judging them because they judged him. Maybe we judge people in an area we are weak in, but do we do it subconsciously? Maybe that makes us feel better about our own shortcomings? I see now that is the wrong way.

Potter got away with keeping the eight thousand dollars, at least in the movie. There may have been an investigation soon. If the police didn't show up at his door and the character was actually real, he would have to answer for it on Judgment Day. Mr. Gower was so fortunate that he did not accidentally cause a death since George prevented it. In either case, we are not the judge.

> "Do not judge others, and you will not be judged. For you will be treated as you treat others. The standard you use in judging is the standard by which you will be judged.
>
> "And why worry about a speck in your friend's eye when you have a log in your own? How can you think of saying to your friend, 'Let me help you get rid of that speck in

your eye,' when you can't see past the log in your own eye? Hypocrite! First get rid of the log in your own eye; then you will see well enough to deal with the speck in your friend's eye. (Matthew 7:1–5)

The LORD himself will fight for you. Just stay calm. (Exodus 14:14)

Cues to Clues to Truths

#36 God will fight for us.

All we need to do is be still and rest in His love and trust Him.

"Show Me the Way, God" by Greg Clark Noir Art

The Further Away From Home I Feel

This is another story of an insensitive son I am ashamed to tell. In 1998, *Saving Private Ryan* hit the theaters. I thought the three generations of Kerley men should go. My teenage son, Dad, and I went to the movies. To this day, I really like the film. I've never served in the military, but I believe it captured the reality of war on the screen and in the sound design.

I thought Dad would love it. It didn't have John Wayne, but this was still a war picture. I think my son liked it okay, but I wish I could take that afternoon back. My poor father was sitting in that theater for almost three hours. I was unaware and inconsiderate to what my father was experiencing. He was almost deaf in his right ear and partially deaf in the other. That being said, at the end of the movie, I finally saw that he had heard everything, seen everything. He was absolutely terrified, and I did that to him. When it was time to leave, I had to stand him up and slowly walk him out. He was paralyzed with fear.

Many veterans say the film's authenticity is remarkably close to the real thing. The film's first thirty minutes depicting the D-Day landing had to be horrible for my father, and I didn't realize until the film was over. It must have recalled bad memories. His brother, Dillard, was killed in action at Tarawa, 11/20/1943. His brother-in-law, Rob, was part of the D-Day Invasion in June 1944. My father served in Korea. The only story he told me of war was one he didn't want to tell or relive.

I was upset about something and believed that I had nothing to live for. For the life of me, I have no idea what was wrong now.

Again, because of my thoughtlessness similar to that movie in 1998, he told me a true story that put life in perspective for me. There is no need to share all the details now, but my father wanted me to know how precious life is, although it hurt him tremendously to tell this story. A buddy of his had been shot, my Dad was resting his friend's head on his lap, holding his brains in place with a helmet. The young Marine was fighting for his life with every breath. Suddenly, I got the point of the story—a point Dad didn't need to relive if only I had been more appreciative and less insensitive.

And in 1998, I put him through the likes of that again. We never spoke of either incident again. As much as I regret knowing both stories were all my fault and cruel treatment to my father, my deepest sorrow is that I didn't adequately apologize. There was no way to take either back. I'm sure there were many times I disappointed my father, but these two transgressions hurt so much because of the way they disappointed me in my actions.

It isn't quite the same thing, but I mention in comparison two things from *It's a Wonderful Life*. The first is Harry's service in World War II and earning the Medal of Honor, and every able-bodied man in Bedford Falls fighting for their country, too. The second is on that Christmas Eve when George's world was crashing down, travel pamphlets and the architectural models he had built in their living room, once good memories, were now devilish reminders. That is how I think of those two stories I shared of how I treated my father. I am so sorry, Dad.

The last paragraph was to be just that, but my friend, Josh, encouraged me to let go of the guilt. Josh reminded me my father is in glory and holds nothing over my head. When Jesus said, "It is finished," all guilt and all shame were destroyed. I found great encouragement in Josh's words. I also laughed with joy when he painted a picture of me entering heaven to find Dad waiting with an extra axe! He had read

"Lightning or Stolen Thunder?" nine stories back, so he wasn't making a comparison to Stanley Kubrick's film, *The Shining*.

> *Praise the LORD, who is my rock. He trains my hands for war and gives my fingers skill for battle. He is my loving ally and my fortress, my tower of safety, my rescuer. He is my shield, and I take refuge in him. He makes the nations submit to me.* (Psalm 144:1–2)

> *Even if my father and mother abandon me, the LORD will hold me close.* (Psalm 27:10)

Cues to Clues to Truths

#37 God will not give up on us.

David knew that God's love and care can go beyond the closest relationships. The world may forsake us, but God will not.

Life Is Just a Leap of Faith

There are a few different ways I could tell this story. Before I begin though, do yourself a favor and listen to Eric Bibb's cover of Guy Clark's song, "The Cape." Go!

If you already know the song, I still hope you listened again. Either way, I hope it touches your heart as it did mine. We each have a different experience, but my wife and I were most fortunate to see Eric Bibb in concert two nights in a row, in two North Carolina towns a few years ago. My wife and I know a sensational younger man by the name of Caleb. The first time I heard "The Cape" with Eric Bibb on the radio, I immediately thought of Caleb. To me, he embodies the song's sentiment and the belief of the hero in the song from little boy to old man.

A leap of faith is the belief in something intangible or incapable of being proved. Think about Noah, Abraham, Moses, David, and Peter. A leap of faith can involve risk, so a blind leap of faith isn't usually sound. With faith in God's Word, we have assurance and counsel. Through His Word, we can find wisdom and direction. The boy, believing he could fly like Superman, trusted his strength was in his cape tied around his neck. There's not much forethought here, but I immediately saw my friend Caleb's courage in the lyrics. He has done some amazing things, and I know it wasn't only because he loved Superman as a child. Before I knew Caleb, I would never attempt his fantastic feats. I am inspired by him and now believe I can do my version of great things, too. We all can, but Caleb would tell you our real strength comes from the Lord.

A helpful cape can be a cape in modern times or a cloak in Jesus's time. In deserts, it can provide protection from strong winds, blowing sand, and the blazing sun. As Caleb reminds me of the little boy jumping off the roof with trust in his cape, he also reminds me of the blind beggar in the Bible. We can throw off our cloak, jump up and run to Jesus, boldly answer his question, and . . .

Follow him.

Other than the actual children of Bedford Falls and Pottersville stories, I guess Clarence was the only one to have the true faith of a child. Mary was confident in what she wanted and could make quick decisions. George made quick decisions, too, and they usually were ones that greatly helped others and thwarted his boyhood plans and desires to travel the world and build skyscrapers, tall buildings, and bridges a mile long. It is poignant how he came to see the light on a small bridge in his hometown.

While George was blind to Clarence at first, he always put himself last with friends and family, but made the right decision for his heart even if it meant his wants and needs were not met. He risked his life for brother Harry and the stranger, Clarence. He and Mary skipped their honeymoon because of the run on the bank. As a boy, he made a difficult decision to help Mr. Gower without his father's assistance. As a father, he tried to fix Zuzu's flower when its petals fell. And when his troubled, absent-minded Uncle Billy lost the Building and Loan's eight thousand dollars, it was George who was determined to take the blame.

At first, he thought his insurance policy was the only way to help his family. After Clarence opened his eyes, the prospect of an innocent man going to prison was worth it to him because he got his family and wonderful life back.

> *Even though the fig trees have no blossoms, and there are no grapes on the vines; even though the olive crop fails, and the fields lie empty and barren; even though the flocks die in the fields, and the cattle barns are empty, yet I will rejoice in the LORD! I will be joyful in the God of my salvation! The Sovereign LORD is my strength! He*

makes me as surefooted as a deer, able to tread upon the heights. (Habakkuk 3:17–19)

Faith is the confidence that what we hope for will actually happen; it gives us assurance about things we cannot see. (Hebrews 11:1)

And Jesus said to him, "Go, for your faith has healed you." Instantly the man could see, and he followed Jesus down the road. (Mark 10:52)

God himself has prepared us for this, and as a guarantee he has given us his Holy Spirit. So we are always confident, even though we know that as long as we live in these bodies we are not at home with the Lord. For we live by believing, and not by seeing. (2 Corinthians 5:5–7)

Search me, O God, and know my heart; test me and know my anxious thoughts. Point out anything in me that offends you, and lead me along the path of everlasting life. (Psalm 139:23–24)

For every child of God defeats this evil world, and we achieve this victory through our faith. (1 John 5:4)

Cues to Clues to Truths

#38 Since believing in Him is the key to being born of God, the key to victory is faith.

This is not only coming to the altar to get saved but a consistent, abiding faith, and an ongoing trust and reliance in Jesus Christ. Because we have faith in Jesus and know what He did for us, we can overcome the world. The trials, the heartaches, the troubling situations, and the schemes of the devil are no match for our God.

Take Up Your Cross

(Dedicated to my brothers from Koloff for Christ Ministries' Man Camp in Royston, Georgia, April 2022: Bill, Casey, Chad, Chris, Chuck, Cory, Donnie, Haus, John R., John W., Josue, Kevin, Marvin, Matthew, Robert, Tom, Trip, and Yellow Fox.)

Luke 9:23 teaches: *"Then he said to the crowd, 'If any of you wants to be my follower, you must give up your own way, take up your cross daily, and follow me.'"*

Whether I knew or acknowledged it at the time, the Lord has brought me through many hardships. Losing loved ones, losing a job and not finding the next one for two years, and all of us going through the Coronavirus Pandemic. I very seldom mention the particularly dark time in my life when I had no job and few prospects of one. I moved to northern Virginia in hopes of employment. The job didn't pan out after a couple of months or so. I felt my mother would have a difficult time without me at home, but it turned out that I was the one struggling over the separation.

I quickly realized I had made the wrong decision for several reasons. I was completely miserable. The job I thought I needed would have had me traveling in various parts of Virginia and the District of Columbia. I was there in October of 2002. Some may recall that was the time of the Washington, D.C. sniper attacks.

I'm ashamed to admit that I was so miserable and lost, that when I would pump gas for my vehicle, I hoped I would be next. I did not mean to trivialize the heartache and grief of so many of those families of victims and also many others across our country. I had lost hope. I was so lost. I had forgotten the One who has always watched over me and cared for me—and loved me.

Fast forward to April 2022, and I am at Man Camp in Royston, Georgia. This spiritual retreat was founded by Nikita Koloff and Lex Luger, two former professional wrestlers I admired. We are about the same age. In fact, Nikita is exactly one day older than me. I joked, "Look at Nikita's accomplishments in life, compare them to mine, and see how much more he was able to do with that one extra day!"

Of course, that one day didn't make any difference. It was how we should approach every day, how we should grow closer to the Lord, and discover what we each can accomplish in His strength. I am most fortunate to have met wonderful men of God in my Man Camp experience. Each of their experiences is an individual one, and I can only speak to my own. This is the glorious part of this story.

Given an opportunity to fast and be alone in nature with our Maker, I had many acres within my reach. I was open to where God was leading me and had no preconceived idea where to go except to avoid the areas I had visited already. In so doing, I remember finding a primitive bench in the woods for my Bible reading and time with God.

After an hour or so, I stood up to take a break. I turned around and saw the bench as something else. I had a vision of the bench as the horizontal beam of Jesus's cross. The two stones supporting each end at first represented the sins Jesus bore for us. Then, I saw them as my sins, and my cross.

In my sixty-four years thus far, God has protected me. This doesn't mean we won't have trials and tribulations, stated in Edwin Louis Cole's book, *Maximized Manhood*. Jesus was willing to die so we might have life. Just as He died on the cross for us, we must die ourselves so that the will of God can be done in our lives.

In all the years I tried to live my life my way, God was still with me. Here is a chorus of a song by Quinton Mills:

"He Never Left Me"

> He never left me, though I turned my back on Him
> Living in a world of sin, trying to run away again
> He never left me, when I chose to walk away
> Even when I couldn't pray, he never left me.

Initially, I thought of George and how he would've missed out on what God had in store for him. Of course, his family and friends would still have their fun memories, but they would have been deprived of opportunities to make more of those with George, had he not asked for help on the bridge.

Then, I thought of Henry Potter. He is the proverbial bad guy in the story. By the end of the movie, we realize George is the *real* richest man in town and never learn what happens to Potter. Some of us hope he is discovered and thrown in jail. Some may not care and assume the old man will rot away all alone.

But just as we are elated when good-natured George comes to his senses and sees he has so many reasons to live, why don't we stop to check in on poor Mr. Potter? He was poor in the ways that George Bailey was wealthy and plentiful. Why can't we deny ourselves and reach out to him? Vengeance is not ours. We are to love others—especially those who might not seem to deserve it.

Read Psalm 51 and reflect on God's unfailing forgiveness and love. David, the psalmist, was human and obviously imperfect. God wants us to be honest, and not make excuses or avoid our responsibilities.

> *For this is how God loved the world: He gave his one and only Son, so that everyone who believes in him will not perish but have eternal life.* (John 3:16)

> *If you refuse to take up your cross and follow me, you are not worthy of being mine. If you cling to your life, you will*

lose it; but if you give up your life for me, you will find it. (Matthew 10:38–39)

For if you live by its dictates, you will die. But if through the power of the Spirit you put to death the deeds of your sinful nature, you will live. (Romans 8:13)

My hands have made both heaven and earth; they and everything in them are mine. I, the LORD, have spoken! "I will bless those who have humble and contrite hearts, who tremble at my word. (Isaiah 66:2)

Cues to Clues to Truths

#39 God responds with grace and mercy if we follow His principles in humility, willingness, and the desire to do what is right while taking up our cross.

To me, taking up our cross, means treating others with respect, setting time aside to study God's Word and practicing discipline daily, but that isn't all. We must have the humility to acknowledge our faults and lay down our weaknesses at the foot of Jesus's cross. We must learn to live in the victory over those weaknesses Jesus paid for when He said, "It is finished." We must be willing to turn from and deal with our wrongs. We must desire to do what is right, no matter how difficult. In our weakness, He makes us strong.

Wandering in the Desert

Reduction in Force, or RIF—believe me, the latter is actually a four-letter word. The bottom line was I lost my job. Back then, that was all I thought I had left. Then, that was gone.

I tried to find another job in the same field, but every lead fell through. When things seemed to get better, it would quickly unravel. Finally, Gaston County gave me a break when no one else would. I'd been without a job for two years. If it hadn't been for dear friends and my sweet mother, I would have been out on the street.

Coming back to the world was not easy. I wish I could say I quickly bounced back through it all. I felt sorry for myself during that desert time and still had anguish when I got what I thought I was missing. I had forgotten that I was the Lord's. I forgot that He was there with me every step of the way. I forgot that He loved me and that He had a purpose for me. When we are between a rock and a hard place, it doesn't mean it's the end.

When I finally got that new job in July of 2003, one day before I was to report, my mother had a stroke. When I saw her, I knew what had happened because Dad had suffered one a while before he passed.

So, I finally had a job, but it was ninety minutes away. I had wanted to be local to look after Mom. Before the stroke, I thought I would commute for a while and then rent an apartment. Then, when her health was failing, I thought maybe I shouldn't take the job. Relatives assured me this was important, and they would help with my dear mother. They definitely did help.

Mom recovered from the stroke and then about eight months later, had to have heart bypass surgery. Then, I thought I would have to drive back and forth a little longer than I originally planned. When my mother went home to Jesus on Thanksgiving Day in 2017, I was still making that three-hour round trip every day.

I kept making that drive until I retired in 2021. I spent a lot of time driving up and down those roads for so many years. Those travels and my forty years wandering in my own desert were for the same reason as for the Israelites. Now think about this, in Deuteronomy 1:2, we learn it was only an eleven-day journey that took them forty years.

My initial journey wouldn't have even been eleven days. All I had to do was turn around and follow my Lord and Savior. Believers are not immune to consequences when we sin. I never lived in a big city, but I quickly learned that was not for me. I like a small-town atmosphere like here in Taylorsville, North Carolina, where my wife, Denise, and I live with our seven cats. I can relate to the small town of Bedford Falls. To their neighborhoods, schools, churches, and families.

George thought he wanted out of Bedford Falls. Mary had been to New York and was homesick. She wanted to come back home to stay. George, for various reasons, did his desert wandering right there in Bedford Falls. It turned out that his little hometown was more than just "not so bad." For him and Mary, it was actually perfect. Mary, like my wife, was much smarter than her husband. My friend and brother, Josh, says about our beautiful, wonderful wives, "We married up!"

> *For I am about to do something new. See, I have already begun! Do you not see it? I will make a pathway through the wilderness. I will create rivers in the dry wasteland.* (Isaiah 43:19)

> *He found them in a desert land, in an empty, howling wasteland. He surrounded them and watched over*

them; he guarded them as he would guard his own eyes. (Deuteronomy 32:10)

This is what the LORD says: "Stop at the crossroads and look around. Ask for the old, godly way, and walk in it. Travel its path, and you will find rest for your souls. But you reply, 'No, that's not the road we want!' (Jeremiah 6:16)

The LORD says, "I will give you back what you lost to the swarming locusts, the hopping locusts, the stripping locusts, and the cutting locusts. It was I who sent this great destroying army against you." (Joel 2:25)

All around him was a glowing halo, like a rainbow shining in the clouds on a rainy day. This is what the glory of the LORD looked like to me. When I saw it, I fell face down on the ground, and I heard someone's voice speaking to me. (Ezekiel 1:28)

If you obey the commands of the LORD your God and walk in his ways, the LORD will establish you as his holy people as he swore he would do. (Deuteronomy 28:9)

Cues to Clues to Truths

#40 God promised the Israelites will be established as His holy people.

Primarily, this is a promise to the faithful who looked to the Lord to give them their promised inheritance of the physical land. Today, God has not promised us a physical land, but an eternal inheritance.

Dillard L. Kerley, USMCR by Over the Moon Photography

"Tarawa, South Pacific, 1943" by Sergeant Tom Lovell, USMC

Tarawa Backwards

My Uncle Dillard died November 20, 1943, at Tarawa. I have studied that WWII battle and know much about how he died, but I know virtually nothing of how he lived. I love him and respect him, and I never knew him. Why then, did it take me so long to love and respect my Lord, and also prove it by my actions?

Tarawa is an atoll in the central Pacific Ocean, now known as the Republic of Kiribati. The island where the U.S. Marines landed was called Betio. To me, the shape of the island looks like a cardinal or blue jay. A lot of things went wrong there. Tides were misjudged. The bombs from Navy ships skipped over the island like smooth rocks on a pond's surface. The Japanese were heavily fortified, and their trained fighting men there were of their best.

The tide was too low when the attack began, which forced many of the landing vehicles to lower their ramps hundreds of yards from the beaches. The Marines had to wade through the reef's shallow water, up to their chest or only knees, and many were picked off during the invasion without reaching their destination. Of the seven beaches, my uncle's battalion landed to one side of a 500-yard pier, on Red Beach 3. I think the pier shown on maps resembles the legs of the island bird. Perhaps my uncle made it to the beach. Regardless, he was one of 1000 Marines who died in the 76-hour battle.

Studying history allows us to observe and learn how people and societies behaved. Winston Churchill wrote, "Those that fail to learn from history are doomed to repeat it." In Matthew 24:6, we learn there will be *"wars and threats of wars."* Yes, these things must take place, but the end won't follow immediately. Tarawa backwards, of course, refers to "a war at?"

In *It's a Wonderful Life*, WWII had ended before that fateful Christmas Eve. There were battles and wars of some type still going on. Life is full of adversity, even in Bedford Falls. There were conflicts at home, stressful jobs, disagreements, and dealing with other people's shortcomings. We know Uncle Billy drank too much. I believe he had self-doubt and missed his wife, Laura. Sometimes we can struggle with life's problems, and there is a challenge to choose what is good for us rather than go down self-destructive paths.

After coming down pretty hard on Uncle Billy, George soon planned to take full responsibility for the loss of the money. I often think of what poor Uncle Billy would have become if George turned his back on him. Whether you are like Uncle Billy, George, Mary, Violet, Harry, Mr. Gower or anyone else in town, share your worry, anxiety, or anger with God. See if your burden doesn't grow lighter.

> *The LORD will mediate between peoples and will settle disputes between strong nations far away. They will hammer their swords into plowshares and their spears into pruning hooks. Nation will no longer fight against nation, nor train for war anymore. Everyone will live in peace and prosperity, enjoying their own grapevines and fig trees, for there will be nothing to fear. The LORD of Heaven's Armies has made this promise!* (Micah 4:3–4)

> *So then, since we have a great High Priest who has entered heaven, Jesus the son of God, let us hold firmly to what we believe. This High Priest of ours understands our weaknesses, for he faced all of the same testings we do, yet he did not sin. So let us come boldly to the throne of our gracious God. There we will receive his mercy, and we will find grace to help us when we need it most.* (Hebrews 4:14–16)

And we know that God causes everything to work together for the good of those who love God and are called according to his purpose for them. (Romans 8:28)

Cues to Clues to Truths

#41 Everything will be all right in the end.

Some things like war, death, divorce, disease, and the Coronavirus pandemic are terrible. Our God is more powerful than all the horrible things that happen in our lives. Even failures and losses somehow become good through Him.

Many a Strife

My father used to tell people he was working on his second million. Surprised, they would ask sarcastically, "Don, are you a millionaire?" He'd reply with a grin, "No, the first million was too hard. That's why I'm working on my second one."

We never became millionaires, but my father and I have a lot in common. Mourning his death, I began a historical fiction novel about his service in the United States Marine Corps. I had a great title, the same as for this chapter, taken from the Marine Corps Hymn. "In many a strife we've fought for life, And never lost our nerve."

I outlined the story that told a partially true rendering of Uncle Dillard and Dad, with fiction continuing with my sons and me. In my novel, we were all Marines. I even enrolled in a weeklong writer's workshop. That is where the dream began to crumble because I couldn't take constructive criticism about it. About twenty years later, my Lord moved me, not to tell a fictitious story, but to tell the stories you are reading now. Stories that really happened. Stories that were funny or tragic. I suppose I could call this chapter, "Many a Strife to a Wonderful Life." He never promised life would be easy. It took me too long to understand it is so much more hopeful when I let Him into my life.

A week before I submitted this manuscript for publishing, I met a fit 80-year-old Marine. I thanked him for his service and that started a long conversation for a South Carolina parking lot in late June. It was well worth it for me.

He joined the Marine Corps in 1964, served in Vietnam, Beirut, and many other locations during his long career. I was blessed with making a new friend and with a story I needed to hear. He told me something he would ask his men, "You know a hard day?" They thought they did.

I am paraphrasing his answer here, but Tony put it much better. I knew I had to add Tony's story to my stories. The best place was here in "Many a Strife." Sergeant Tony would tell his men, "A hard day is wearing a helmet of thorns, rucking a 200-lb. pack on your back, humping that gear for a mile hike after a long beating, with no rations, no canteen, with people shouting and spitting at you, wanting you dead, your hands and feet pierced to hang you on a post to die from suffocation, shock, exhaustion, or just bleeding to death, and then, sacrificing your life for something someone else did. *That* was a hard day! Do not tell me anything you do is hard!"

Semper Fi, Sergeant!

In *It's a Wonderful Life*, there is much strife in the day-to-day living of people who survived the Great Depression and the Second World War. I am not saying that George was God, but I believe God used George just as He can use all of us to carry out His work, and do great things through Him. Even in tragedy and pain, God can make a miracle.

Harry broke through the ice at the age of nine, but went on to be a football star and later won the Medal of Honor. Mr. Gower grieved over the loss of his son and made a terrible mistake, but he carried on without crawling inside a bottle. Peter Bailey had frequent quarrels with Mr. Potter, but in his last night on earth, he and his son had a heart-to-heart talk. Ernie was a simple man making a living while driving a taxi, but Bedford Falls' Ernie kept his family together and was encouraged by great friendships with Bert the cop and George the banker.

Come to think of it, the teenage prank of revealing the swimming pool lurking underneath the dance floor could have led to disaster. Instead, students and faculty had a big dance night they would never forget. George and Mary shared a special evening. I think it would have been nice if George could have gone to see his father after the stroke, but not let that pull the young couple apart. Then, I remembered our plans don't always match God's plan.

George got a second chance in life just as I did in my writing. As I write this, I know I could never have attempted such a thing without my parents, Denise, Josh, and my many friends, and most importantly, my Lord and Savior.

> *What is causing the quarrels and fights among you? Don't they come from the evil desires at war within you? You want what you don't have, so you scheme and kill to get it. You are jealous of what others have, but you can't get it, so you fight and wage war to take it away from them. Yet you don't have what you want because you don't ask God for it. And even when you ask, you don't get it because your motives are all wrong—you want only what will give you pleasure.* (James 4:1–3)

> *The LORD himself watches over you! The LORD stands beside you as your protective shade.* (Psalm 121:5)

Cues to Clues to Truths

#42 God is our eternal keeper.

God protects us through any calamity.

Tradition Permission–and Grace

My father-in-law, Bill, was a great man. The one regret I have in my relationship with him is that I didn't follow through on my intent to ask his permission to marry his daughter. There were certain reasons that clouded my judgment, but I should've still honored and respected him, while I continued to be mindful of health issues and other sources of stress.

Some people say it is an old-fashioned custom. Others would say it doesn't matter, but it's still tradition. I was in my fifties and had been married once before. Denise was seven years younger and had never wed. I believe it's still necessary to ask for permission or blessing for the daughter's hand in marriage.

Opinions on this range from a sweet way to include the parents to an antiquated practice that should be phased out. Some may believe it is insulting to the bride. Traditional parents may be offended if not asked. Even if they aren't traditional, it's a nice idea to at least clue them in that the couple is thinking about marriage. If happily married, I think they should be asked together. If divorced, then ask each individually.

Let them know you are sincere and a gentleman. Talk to your girlfriend first, and plan together what each of you want to happen and how to go about this important step. Promise him you will take care of his daughter. Ask her parents for advice on marriage. Their experience is invaluable. Allow her parents to ask you questions.

I admit I didn't do this. I knew right away it was a mistake, but my father-in-law never treated me differently because of it. His health wasn't good, and we hoped and prayed he'd be able to walk their daughter down the aisle. The Lord provided that just as we had hoped, but I knew I'd made a mistake in not talking to him about my intentions and about how much I loved his daughter.

My father-in-law died too soon. I didn't have him long enough, and I know his son and daughter miss him deeply. So, this may seem like advice I am giving that I didn't properly take or address. As I write this, I know I should've asked both Bill and Margaret for permission to marry Denise. Bill is in heaven now, and Margaret is still living. I pray they are both happy with their son-in-law. I broke a tradition, but both my in-laws always extended to me nothing but love, care, understanding—and grace. I must do the same.

George didn't really propose properly, let alone ask for Mary's hand in marriage. Mary had known since she was a child how she felt about George. George didn't really see this as a young boy. At the dance, he perhaps truly saw her for the first time. Then, his father died that night, and he continued to do what he had to do, but every time, what he wanted seemed to grow further from his reach.

Then, the night George went for a walk, he spoke briefly with Violet, but it was evident that they wanted different things in life. He then found himself at the Hatch residence. Rather than knocking on the door, he paced back and forth at the gate.

We want George and Mary to fall in love. Things seemed to be moving in that direction, then something always happened. Mary played their song on the record player. George thought she was teasing him. Maybe if she made him jealous, he would admit he liked her? Everything seemed to backfire on them both.

Now, if George had asked her mother to marry her daughter, what would she have said? Remember, Mary's mother thought the successful Sam Wainwright was who her daughter should marry. She didn't seem to consider what Mary wanted but only what she thought was best. And on their wedding day, it was a downpour. Mrs. Hatch was so sad that her daughter was in love with the wrong man. Even if asked, she may not have given her blessing. Through the years though, I have to believe that George won at least some respect from his mother-in-law.

> *So give your father and mother joy! May she who gave you birth be happy.* (Proverbs 23:25)

> *There are three things that amaze me—no, four things that I don't understand: how an eagle glides through the sky, how a snake slithers on a rock, how a ship navigates the ocean, how a man loves a woman.* (Proverbs 30:18–19)

> *Always be humble and gentle. Be patient with each other, making allowance for each other's faults because of your love. Make every effort to keep yourselves united in the Spirit, binding yourselves together with peace.* (Ephesians 4:2–3)

> *Each time he said, "My grace is all you need. My power works best in weakness." So now I am glad to boast about my weaknesses, so that the power of Christ can work through me. That's why I take pleasure in my weaknesses, and in the insults, hardships, persecutions, and troubles that I suffer for Christ. For when I am weak, then I am strong.* (2 Corinthians 12:9–10)

Cues to Clues to Truths

#43 God gives us grace.

Life on this earth involves hardship and difficult decisions. God proclaimed that His grace can provide everything we need to endure life's suffering and our occasional misjudgments.

It's a Sin to Kill a Mockingbird

I chose to present this story a little differently. For a creative writing assignment online, I was asked to write some dialogue. Having just auditioned for a play, *The Shawshank Redemption*, by Owen O'Neill and Dave Johns, I'd seen a talented young man whom I had worked with before in another theater's production of *To Kill a Mockingbird*. Something that happened in that production had bothered me for years, but I'd never straightened it out. Even years later, I couldn't find my way to simply come out and say what was bothering me. I wrote this dialogue to give to Jordan on the night of our script table-read. I would be the second guard, and Jordan was cast as Red. Rather than tell him bravely, I put my thoughts down in my dialogue assignment for him to read. My assignment and plea to a friend is below:

Jordan's eyes lit up Monday night when he saw David at auditions. David told him how happy he'd been to follow his progress in community theater through the years, since their last show together. On the following Monday, both cast in *The Shawshank Redemption*, David was granted another chance to tell Jordan what was on his heart.

"Hey, David! Congratulations! I believed we'd get to do this show together!"

"Yeah, buddy, I hoped we would, too. I knew you would be Red! . . . Uh, Jordan, there's something I need to talk with you about, something that has bothered me for years."

Seeing the seriousness in his face, "Sure, David. What's wrong?"

"The last time I saw you before auditions last week, we were in *To Kill a Mockingbird* together.

Jordan nodded.

"I owe you an apology, Jordan."

"What for?"

"Well, in my process of method acting as the prosecuting attorney, I went too far with you being on trial in the play."

Jordan was more puzzled now, but continued to give his friend the time to explain why he was upset.

"Uh, you see, I have regretted for years, me whispering to you during the show, 'Your lawyer can't even protect his own family. How do you expect him to protect you?'"

"Why did that bother you?"

With eyes glistening, "That meant I was looking down on you. Lots of actors like playing the bad guy, but I hated it. Maybe I wasn't as bad as Ewell, but I didn't like what I did to you. You didn't deserve that. Your character didn't either. It wasn't in the script, and it was wrong of me even if the audience didn't hear it . . . 'It's a sin to kill a mockingbird.'"

Jordan wrapped his arms around the older man. "Brother, you didn't hurt this mockingbird one bit." With a big smile, "But you can shoot all the blue jays you want!"

I gave the exercise in dialogue to Jordan, and I hope he understood what I was trying to say. In *Shawshank*, we again were on different sides, but it felt much more comfortable this time around. I think we shared a bond. He is a special man, and it was an honor to be on stage with him.

Just as there are some innocent men in prison, there are also guilty ones on the outside. Prison and plays aside, we all are going through something. It may be a difficult time that no one understands or ever knows about. In Stephen King's story, we learn to, "Get busy living, or get busy dying."

Are people essentially good or essentially evil? I thought about that question and considered what Mr. Potter said to George. "You're worth more dead than alive! Why don't you go to the riffraff you love so much and ask them to let you have eight thousand dollars? You know why? Because they'd run you out of town on a rail. But I'll tell you what I'm going to do for you, George. Since the state examiner is still here, as a stockholder of the Building and Loan, I'm going to swear out a warrant for your arrest. Misappropriation of funds, manipulation, malfeasance! *(George exits.)* All right, George, go ahead! You can't hide in a little town like this!"

Potter deemed the townspeople disreputable, undesirable, and worthless. To him, they were riffraff. But for the most part, they were people who had problems like all of us and chose to keep on keeping on, the best way they could. And don't forget, the only crime we see committed is when Henry Potter kept the eight thousand dollars that Uncle Billy mistakenly folded into the newspaper. Even when George asks for a loan to pay the money back, Potter still didn't admit his responsibility in the matter. He is surprised to hear George say he lost the money. As far as we know, Potter never did confess. Potter knew who'd lost the money and refused to come clean when George took the blame to protect his uncle. Who actually displayed true character?

> *What sorrow for those who say that evil is good and good is evil, that dark is light and light is dark, that bitter is sweet and sweet is bitter.* (Isaiah 5:20)

> *Don't just pretend to love others. Really love them. Hate what is wrong. Hold tightly to what is good.* (Romans 12:9)

> *And everyone present was filled with the Holy Spirit and began speaking in other languages, as the Holy Spirit gave them this ability.* (Acts 2:4)

> *A person who strays from home is like a bird that strays from its nest. The heartfelt counsel of a friend is as sweet*

> *as perfume and incense. Never abandon a friend—either yours or your father's. When disaster strikes, you won't have to ask your brother for assistance. It's better to go to a neighbor than to a brother who lives far away.* (Proverbs 27:8–10)

> *He has given me a new song to sing, a hymn of praise to our God. Many will see what he has done and be amazed. They will put their trust in the LORD.* (Psalm 40:3)

> *I tell you the truth, those who listen to my message and believe in God who sent me have eternal life. They will never be condemned for their sins, but they have already passed from death into life.* (John 5:24)

Cues to Clues to Truths

#44 The Cross of Calvary provides victory over death.

Souls who choose to live sinfully and never repent will suffer a second death while those who put trusting faith in Christ will be with God forever.

Uncle Dave Scott

My best friend is Josh Scott. Since his three children were young, they have always called me Uncle Dave. Today, two are married, the youngest will graduate from college in 2024, and I am still family to all of them.

I suppose that would not have happened if their father and I weren't so close. God brought Josh and me together years ago. I believe we were connected long before we actually met. God knew we needed each other. We both have many friends, but there's something very special in our friendship. We think of ourselves as brothers, and we both need to connect through texts every day, and the occasional phone call. We pray for each other. We lift each other up. We listen and we encourage. Josh knew the day I bought Denise a ring and the day I gave it to her. He stood by me as my Best Man on our wedding day. This tight bond has gone on since soon after we met, and his wife, Gina, and their children—Kiersten, Isaiah, and Elijah treat me accordingly.

About three years ago, my wife and I, along with Josh and Gina, Elijah and his girlfriend, Ragan, went to the Billy Graham Center in Asheville, North Carolina, to see Jason Crabb in concert. Standing in line for the buffet before the concert, Josh reflected on their children calling me Uncle Dave. "You gave them something and said, 'This is from your Uncle Dave, and since then they've always called you that. You're family!'"

I remembered then exactly what he was talking about, for I had won a Wii gaming system and had given it to them. However, I didn't recall I had given myself that nickname. It hurt a little that I may have coaxed it, but then I began to examine the memory and saw how me saying that one time couldn't have made three siblings automatically usher me into their family. It wasn't about greed either. They are fine people, and I am proud of each of them.

Kiersten is a nurse, Isaiah is a Youth and Young Adult Associate Pastor, and Elijah studied Psychology at North Greenville University where Josh teaches. For a brief time, we all lived within thirty minutes of each other, but they have since lived in Virginia, two areas in the great state of Texas, and now members of the family are in South Carolina and Colorado. Kirsten and her husband, Aidan, live in South Carolina, as do Josh and Gina, and Isaiah and his wife, Gabby, reside in Colorado. Elijah and Ragan will marry after his graduation in 2024.

I grew up as an only child, and I think of the children who are now adults as my niece and nephews. Even if I had lots of brothers and sisters who had several children, the Scott children would still be my family, too. You can't choose your family, but having a family choose you is mighty special. It should not be taken for granted. Gina Scott says about me, "His last name may not be Scott, but he will always be a Scott to us."

How do you remember Uncle Billy? Was he the forgetful drunkard who carelessly lost eight thousand dollars to the most evil man in Bedford Falls and put the Bailey Building and Loan, and George, in jeopardy? Can we blame only Uncle Billy, or shouldn't we see that if he'd misplaced the money in a hundred different ways, the money would've been turned in by honest townspeople and the crisis averted?

Yes, Uncle Billy drank. Yes, he was absent-minded, so much so, that he resorted to tying strings around his fingers to help him remember. Sadly, that never seemed to work.

Remember the scene when George is in a rage with Uncle Billy over the missing money? I understand George's state of mind, but my heart breaks for Billy Bailey. Once in the film he mentions losing Laura, his wife. Pay attention to Uncle Billy's menagerie he had. Someone like my wife who loves animals that much is a very kind and caring person.

Did he really deserve his reputation and tough breaks? Which hard to remember memory would stay with him longer—George calling him an old fool in a rage or later discovering that his nephew contemplated suicide in his taking the blame for Billy's mistake?

Now, think about us. How are we like Uncle Billy? There is good and bad in all of us. Don't we hope that others see at least a glimmer of good that makes us worthwhile? And if we think we don't make mistakes like Uncle Billy . . . well, maybe we aren't paying enough attention to what's really going on.

There was only one perfect man, and He died for all our sins. Where would we be without Jesus?

> *This is my commandment: Love each other in the same way I have loved you. There is no greater love than to lay down one's life for one's friends.* (John 15:12–13)
>
> *Therefore, whenever we have the opportunity, we should do good to everyone—especially to those in the family of faith.* (Galatians 6:10)
>
> *Jesus called out to them, "Come, follow me, and I will show you how to fish for people!"* (Mark 1:17)

Cues to Clues to Truths

#45 We will bring more people to God.

We are to follow the teachings of Jesus, so that the love of God can be seen in us. Through us, then, people will start to turn to God, also.

"Zuzu's Petals, Bert!" by Greg Clark Noir Art

Everyone's Best Friend

If the Lord grants me my next birthday here on earth, I will be sixty-five in 2024. These days, my prayer life is healthier than it has ever been, but it still needs more from me. I read the Word more than I ever have before, but I still miss some days or don't sometimes focus enough on what God must be trying to say to me in that passage. It may sound like it, but I am not bragging. I'm admitting it took me over six decades to do this. What if I never had that many chances? Don't wait as long as I did. Don't wait until tomorrow to make a decision because tomorrow may never come.

Aside from prayer and reading my Bible, if I ever was in a jam, I needed my father or my best friend, Randy. Even when Dad died, every day for months I would say to myself, "I need to tell Dad this," "Dad will know what to do," or "Wait until my Daddy hears this!" Something good or bad would happen, and I needed to take it to him. And for a second, I believed I could.

Randy was the same way. He was my friend. He rejoiced with me in good news. He was there to listen when my heart was breaking. When I needed a favor, Randy was the one I went to if Dad couldn't help. Often, Randy was the one I chose because I didn't want Dad to know what stupid or careless thing I had done.

Here is just one of those examples. I was hauling items to the basement of my first house that wasn't my parents. It was after a long rain, but I didn't concern myself with that. Having unloaded, now it was time to get out of the backyard, which sloped downhill from the basement. I quickly became stuck in the mud, but I believed that I could fix it. I backed up and then tried to go forward, hopefully getting in a position where I could drive out of there.

As you may have guessed, in a few minutes, I found myself at the bottom of the hill after having torn up the yard. I called Randy to tell him what I'd done. "Randy, I thought I could get out of the mud, but if I keep on like I am, I will end up in the creek!" Randy quickly came to my aid and saved my vehicle from its muddy prison. He didn't tell me I should've called him before it got as bad as it did, but he would've been right.

He was there for me when my son, Michael, died. Randy was the one who hitched his trailer to his truck, and drove north to Virginia with me to retrieve my belongings when a job went south. I had paid rent for three months for a place in another state I had run away from because I dreaded going back there so badly.

When my dad was alive, I vividly remember him saying he was glad I had a friend like Randy. In high school, college, and for so many years, Randy was my best friend. What I finally began to realize then and certainly know now is: I am not the only one who believes that. Many people think of Randy as their best friend because of all he has done for them. Isn't that the way we all should live?

This comparison is easy. This time it is my friend, Randy, and George Bailey. They both sacrificed their wishes for others. They did most of the work so others could look good. They pitched in to help people out of a jam, not caring what was in it for them.

The difference between them is that Randy always seemed happy and content every day, no matter what was happening. George Bailey may have been the richest man in town, but the people of my hometown were made richer just because they knew Randy. How many of us, if we were honest, can say that?

> *There is no greater love than to lay down one's life for one's friends* (John 15:13)

Wounds from a sincere friend are better than many kisses from an enemy. (Proverbs 27:6)

A friend is always loyal, and a brother is born to help in time of need. (Proverbs 17:17)

Don't be selfish; don't try to impress others. Be humble, thinking of others as better than yourselves. Don't look out only for your own interests, but take an interest in others, too. (Philippians 2:3–4)

Each time he said, "My grace is all you need. My power works best in weakness." So now I am glad to boast about my weaknesses, so that the power of Christ can work through me. That's why I take pleasure in my weaknesses, and in the insults, hardships, persecutions, and troubles that I suffer for Christ. For when I am weak, then I am strong. (2 Corinthians 12:9–10)

Cues to Clues to Truths

#46 God will strengthen us.

In God's grace and our humility, as we are weakened by difficulties, He will always give us strength.

Live Like Saul or Die Like Paul?

This was my next to last memoir story written, but I chose to place it here before the final three. It's the only one that was presented to me in a dream. Dreams are interesting to me, but I often don't remember mine very well, if at all. This one stuck with me.

When I do recall a dream, it often has to do with work, even though I am retired. Or I am in a situation that isn't very pleasant. I imagine stress and anxiety trigger such nightmares. A major change in your life can do the same thing.

This particular dream was different. I dreamed I was listening to Daniel preach. I do like time travel stories, but in this dream, I believe I was a regular person about 535 BC, listening to Daniel from the Bible. Remember how God showed Daniel the king's dream in a vision and taught him what it meant? I think He was again trying to get my attention. This guy who said God didn't talk to him but knew He spoke to others, is beginning to see He was talking and teaching in many ways, but I failed to listen, see, and understand most of the time.

People will say Daniel didn't preach as Paul did. However, his life, beliefs, and explanation of prophetic dreams and visions do preach to me. I believe Daniel can be seen as a prophet just as Paul was an apostle. I also believe God gave me that dream about Daniel, and Daniel gave me this insight into Paul.

As I was waking from the dream, the thought of Paul preaching came into my mind. I imagined having the opportunity and blessing to hear directly from Paul. Just as quickly, I began to think of the opposite message I would receive if I were listening to the thoughts and beliefs of Saul.

Of course, Saul and Paul were entirely the same person, but their thoughts, objectives, actions, and words were totally different. Before his conversion, Saul opposed the followers of Jesus and wished to end the spread of the gospel. He persecuted those followers. But you see, God had other plans for him. Then, something important happened on his way to Damascus.

Saul, also known as Paul, later became one of the most influential believers in the history of Christianity. Paul was converted and called to follow Jesus in a bold way. There's much more to this story of Saul/Paul as you probably already know.

I had always thought Saul's name was changed to Paul as Abram had been changed to Abraham and Jacob to Israel. Researching now, I see he was always Saul and always Paul. That is my personal connection to this story. What if a non-believer heard me speak? Or what if they observed my actions or how I treated others?

That may be their only impression of who God is, just through a direct or indirect encounter with me or any one of us. Let's face it, we don't always behave as we wish we would. The difference in me and Paul is that I sometimes go back and forth. That shouldn't be the case, but it is true.

Now, think about a time when you behaved badly or hurt someone. That is not what Christians should do. I could blame mine on someone else or quickly rationalize my behavior being the result of a bad day, week, or year. That would be wrong. How we carry out every day is important in our walk with Jesus Christ, but it is also critical to live in example to others who look up to you as well as those who are merely watching. Don't allow us to lead anyone astray.

With those thoughts processing still in our minds, think about Mary, then George, and finally Henry Potter from *It's a Wonderful Life*. Mary was always pure in her ways, as far as I can recall from the movie. George usually said and did the right thing when it came down to it, but not always with the right frame of mind and not always for the right reasons. Now, consider Potter. He rarely, if at all, did what was just. He believed he was better than others. He seemed to only care about himself.

If people look up to George or Mary, they may choose to behave similarly to them. If Potter was their role model, they may actually become worse than he ever was. I'm not saying that people can't change, but we should change for the better. And we sometimes backslide. Then, we must confess, repent, accept consequences, and move forward with God.

> *We can rejoice, too, when we run into problems and trials, for we know that they help us develop endurance. And endurance develops strength of character, and character strengthens our confident hope of salvation. And this hope will not lead to disappointment. For we know how dearly God loves us, because he has given us the Holy Spirit to fill our hearts with his love.* (Romans 5:3–5)

> *Therefore, dear brothers and sisters, you have no obligation to do what your sinful nature urges you to do. For if you live by its dictates, you will die. But if through the power of the Spirit you put to death the deeds of your sinful nature, you will live. For all who are led by the Spirit of God are children of God.* (Romans 8:12–14)

> *For I swear, dear brothers and sisters, that I face death daily. This is as certain as my pride in what Christ Jesus our Lord has done in you.* (1 Corinthians 15:31)

> *This means that anyone who belongs to Christ has become a new person. The old life is gone; a new life has begun!* (2 Corinthians 5:17)

> *And now I am bound by the spirit to go to Jerusalem. I don't know what awaits me, except that the Holy Spirit tells me in city after city that jail and suffering lie ahead. But my life is worth nothing to me unless I use it for finishing the work assigned me by the Lord Jesus—the work of telling others the Good News about the wonderful grace of God.* (Acts 20:22–24)

> *So I say, let the Holy Spirit guide your lives. Then you won't be doing what your sinful nature craves.* (Galatians 5:16)

Cues to Clues to Truths

#47 Walking in the Spirit means that the Holy Spirit lives in us, being open and sensitive to the influence of the Holy Spirit, and patterning our lives accordingly.

The Holy Spirit doesn't move in us to gratify our sinful desires but to guide us in the path of Jesus.

Let Her Who Bore You Rejoice

This is my first and only book. My beginner's technique was to fill three journals with my handwritten stories before typing the first word in my manuscript. Off and on, I wrote for a year, but I had the most success in the beginning. Maybe those were easier stories to tell.

When I was typing and reading my stories again in the second year, I saw that there were three pairs of similar stories. Two stories were about my one-person show for Christmas, and two were about Denise. They were similar but different enough to keep them in the book.

The other stories were both about Mother's final week on this earth, and they were almost identical. When I'd written the second story and realized I had put down the same things months before, the only real difference were the titles of the stories. I felt I must remedy the second parallel story by telling about Mom's stroke and heart surgery, but I found that I mentioned those events in "Wandering in the Desert." Then, I remembered many stories of my dear mother making sacrifices for me, and a few more events stood out.

I always had a long workday every day with the commute and inspections to conduct. One day, I'd planned to work late as I had some assigned facilities that didn't open until 5:00 pm. About that time, Mom called me to say she'd locked herself out of the house. She said she was fine and that she was at Gene's house—her gentleman friend after my father died. I reminded her that I had a late inspection to conduct if it was still okay with her. She assured me it was. I thought little about it if they had just begun their visit together and followed through with my inspection and then drove to Taylorsville from the restaurant.

I went to pick her up from Gene's and that was when I discovered that she had been locked out since that morning, not since 5:00 in the evening. She hadn't wanted to bother me. She had kept it a secret as long as she could.

Another time, she told Gene's two grandsons who lived next door to him, "Let's race to your house!" to get there before their grandfather drove his truck to the next driveway. They took off and on her second step or so, she fell to the ground.

I was working in Virginia at the time. She called me and said she did something dumb. She explained about the short race and stated she was fine. I had a bad feeling it wasn't fine in the least. As it turned out, I unfortunately was correct. Her shoulder was broken. I came home to take care of her, not just for that reason, but because I missed her so much. I had thought she would have a terrible time missing me, but she had done well. I was the one who was miserable being apart.

Oh, and another time, I came home from work after I'd finally found the job to complete my career that God had chosen for me. She met me at the door, and I immediately knew something was wrong. She leaned in for a hug with the saddest face I could remember. I noticed that her leg was awkwardly out to one side. When I asked, she lifted her foot to reveal a hole torn in the flooring of our kitchen. She had tried to clean out the dust bunnies from behind the refrigerator, and my tiny mother moving the refrigerator had dug into the floor. Asking her what would have happened had the thing fallen on her, she replied, "I guess I would be there when you got home."

After Denise and I were married and living with Mom, we awoke to a terrible noise. Mom had gotten up in the night for a sip of soda, she later believed she had dozed off while standing at the counter and fallen backwards to the floor. Dee noticed right away by the placement of one of her legs, her hip was most likely broken. Unfortunately, Dee was correct. If someone felt Mom was being punished for her wrongs, then they had the same misguided beliefs of Job's friends. Suffering still happens to believers.

Read the stories again about Mom's stroke and bypass surgery, and about her last week before finally going home. Read "Chicken Neck Delicacy" and see that it's also about her raising her child the way her mom had raised her and her brothers and sister. I have lots of stories I used to tell that were funny about Mom, but they just don't seem appropriate here. They probably never were. I used to tell them, and they always got big laughs. I realized too late they weren't funny to her, and now they aren't funny to me either. Referring to the title, we can all agree that my mother was the one who did what the Bible verse describes, not me. I'm trying to join my mother and correct that.

It is true there is no exact correlation of my story with *It's a Wonderful Life*, but there are, of course, several parent-child relationships. Think of how distraught Mr. Gower was when his son died of the flu, and when he became more upset, he slapped George repeatedly on his sore ear. Remember old maid Mary living a much different life in Pottersville without her husband and children.

Then, picture the bitter, old hag at Ma Bailey's Boarding House. She had lost her son, Harry, and her husband, Peter. This mother seemed to have nothing left. Truly, George, wasn't the only factor here. Maybe parents get some things wrong from time to time, but it's possible to fulfill your own life as a parent and, at the same time, do the same for your children. It really is a two-way street of love and respect.

> *But those who won't care for their relatives, especially those in their own household, have denied the true faith. Such people are worse than unbelievers.* (1 Timothy 5:8)

> *"Honor your father and mother, as the LORD your God commanded you. Then you will live a long, full life in the land the LORD your God is giving you.* (Deuteronomy 5:16)

> *Let your father and mother be glad; let her who bore you rejoice.* (Proverbs 23:25 ESV)

> *The LORD directs the steps of the godly. He delights in every detail of their lives. Though they stumble, they will never fall, for the LORD holds them by the hand.* (Psalm 37:23–24)

Cues to Clues to Truths

#48 God will make our steps firm.

He promises to help us take firm steps so that we will make the right decisions in whatever challenges life may give us.

Life Is Wonderful

This may have been my hardest story to write. Some others were difficult because they dealt with tragic events from the past, or how I poorly handled a situation. This one is hard because I know I could try and try and never capture the true beauty in this story.

This is about my bride, Denise. I had been married before, and that marriage ended in divorce a few years after my older son died. Dee had been engaged once before, but she'd never married. We both had reached a point in our lives where we said, "Huh! I didn't think I would end up alone." We didn't feel sorry for ourselves. We just accepted it.

The funny thing is we both had mutual friends in community theater but had never met or been introduced. Finally, I heard her name, Denise (Dee) Ballerini and that stuck with me. Our paths would eventually cross.

I was Assistant Director for a show called *Flaming Idiots*. Dee and her friend, Amber, came to see the show to support friends of theirs in the cast. Here was my chance. After they took their seats, I left the box office to take them awards ballots to evaluate their favorite actors. I've never been able to charm a stranger, so I don't know how I thought that would work. I just knew I had to try something, but it didn't take.

The next week, rehearsals began for *A Christmas Carol*. We had both been cast in smaller character roles. She and her friend, Jill, were the two thieves with Old Joe, and I was one of the philanthropists with my friend, Marshall. At rehearsals, I tried again to get her attention, but failed miserably.

One day, I felt someone tap my left shoulder, and I turned but no one was there. Then, I would feel a tap on my right shoulder, and no one was there again. I eventually caught on and realized it was her. It gave me some much-needed confidence. We were able to talk some at rehearsals with other people around. We finally got to talk alone after rehearsal one night, and that was the best time I had had in a long time. When I ran out of things to say, I said, "This was fun. I hope we can go out sometime." With a sly grin, she said, "I gave you my number last week."

Okay, so I had obviously dropped the ball. I still wasn't sure she was interested though. That is why I say I met her at *Flaming Idiots*, and she met me at *A Christmas Carol*.

Our first date was December 11, 2011, the Sunday after our show closed. We went to see a play at Hibriten High School, *Christmas Belles*. One of our friends, Nick, was in that show, and he had told Denise, after I had unsettled her by a dumb remark I made, that I really was a good guy. I say we wouldn't be married if it weren't for Nick Clark, and she says our marriage is all our director Beth's fault for casting us.

We both soon knew that we were meant to be a couple. I thought I was clever to use the three-word phrase, "Life is wonderful." I vaguely explained that for many years, I hadn't been happy. She had begun to teach me just how wonderful my life truly was, and she made everything better. "Life is wonderful. Do you know what I mean by those three words?" Her reply was, "I love you, too."

It wasn't until January 28, 2023, when we watched *The Princess Bride* with 500 strangers and got to meet Cary Elwes, that I realized I had actually copied Westley from *The Princess Bride*. His "As you wish" and my "Life is wonderful" mean the same thing. My wise wife had to know all along. She arranged to play *The Princess Bride* instrumental music while seating guests and the song, "Storybook Love" while her dad led the bride to her groom on February 23, 2013.

How was it possible that it took me so long to realize my statement was unoriginal? I hear you all saying: "Inconceivable!" To that

I say, "Mawwiage . . . mawwiage is wot bwings us twogether twoday. Mawwiage, that bwessed awwangement, that dweam wifin a dweam and wuv, twu wuv, wiw fowwow you foweva. So tweasure your wuv."

As I tweasure mine. Now, back to our time getting to know each other. After several months together–together, I bought a ring. Those two togethers are not a mistake. You see, when Dee told Nick Clark we were going to see him in his play together, he asked with wide eyes and a big smile, "Together–together?" So ever since then, both of us repeated that word anytime we were as one. My first "I love you" to the one I wanted to spend the rest of my life with wasn't very bold, so I knew the way I asked her to marry me had to be special and memorable.

We went to our favorite theater, Barter in Abingdon, Virginia, to see a play, *Avenue Q*. My plan was to ask her to marry me at dinner before the play. Dinner at The Peppermill was good, but there was an older couple seated directly beside us, and I was too nervous to go into my special proposal. I then decided to ask her after the show instead.

If you aren't familiar with that play, I will say the actors performed holding puppets who were the real stars of the show. Quickly, the magic of theater made you believe the actors weren't there and that the puppets were real and actually presenting the story all by themselves.

On Denise's left was the sponsor of the show who also had a puppet, and the puppet clapped for the puppets on stage. That was a little different, I must admit. On her right was me, with the ring box in my pocket. In the play, the main character has been looking for his purpose in life. At one point, the word, *Purpose*, was shown on a screen. It became blurry, and the letters began to wiggle. Then, the word, Purpose, changed to the word, *Propose*. That freaked me out a bit. However, I had no puppet and, besides, I still had my special proposal that I wasn't able to unveil at dinner.

After the play, when it was just the two of us, together–together, I began my own one act play. In it, similar to the solo show I would perform a decade later, I became the various characters of *It's a Wonderful Life*. In my Jimmy Stewart impression, I was George Bailey asking my

Mary if she would marry me. Some of you might like to know exactly what I said and the various characters I portrayed, but other than me and my lovely bride, her mother is the only one who has the words to my original script. I believe we will keep that to ourselves.

To hear Denise tell it though, she would simply say, "David performed this ten-minute play... and in the middle of it, I realized he was going to propose." Yes, that was my intent. I mean purpose, just as in *Avenue Q*. Life has been even more wonderful ever since. All because I met that one person that made me forget about yesterday and dream about tomorrow.

Mary Hatch Bailey was a special lady. Out of all the people in Bedford Falls, she seems to be the most content in her own skin and the kindest person she could be in every situation. Even when George is distraught on Christmas Eve, she protects her children and gets her husband's attention by saying, "Why must you torture the children, why don't you . . ." Mary doesn't finish her sentence, and George stumbles out the door. While George encounters Clarence, Mr. Welch, and Nick the bartender, Mary is working hard to alert all family and friends that George is in trouble.

There are other couples in the story, too. George's parents seemed to have a good marriage, and they raised two fine sons. George's brother, Harry, marries Ruth, whom he met at college, and takes a job working for her father. George is disappointed initially that now Harry is married, and George had expected him to come home and run the Building and Loan. He sees they are very much in love and decides not to stand in their way.

Another couple you don't get to see, is Uncle Billy and his wife, Laura. Her name is only mentioned once, but he loved her very much. Dealing with life without her in it was extremely difficult for him. I believe his array of interesting pets, his job at the Bailey Brothers Building and Loan, and his two nephews kept him going.

Two people are better off than one, for they can help each other succeed. (Ecclesiastes 4:9)

The man who finds a wife finds a treasure, and he receives favor from the LORD. (Proverbs 18:22)

For I know the plans I have for you," says the LORD. "They are plans for good and not for disaster, to give you a future and a hope. In those days when you pray, I will listen. If you look for me wholeheartedly, you will find me. (Jeremiah 29:11–13)

"For the mountains may move and the hills disappear, but even then my faithful love for you will remain. My covenant of blessing will never be broken," says the LORD, who has mercy on you. (Isaiah 54:10)

Cues to Clues to Truths

#49 Our God gives us unfailing, faithful, never-ending love.

His love isn't dependent upon our performance and not based on our faithfulness. His love is faithful and never-ending regardless of who we are or what we've done.

Transformers

On December 2, 2021, I was fortunate to perform a one-person show of *This Wonderful Life* by Steve Murray. It allowed me to portray all the characters of Bedford Falls from the film, *It's a Wonderful Life*, even the ladies and children. The play's premise is that the actor loves the movie so much that he wants to perform the entire story for the audience. That part was easy. I do love that movie that much.

The difficult part at first was learning the lines. It is seventy-five minutes of material but when you are the sole actor, the load is on your shoulders with no input from an ensemble. I was the ensemble. I had always memorized my previous roles quite early, but they weren't this complex. Not just in recalling the lines, but I had to think who I was portraying in that particular moment and deliver the lines in the correct voice with the mannerisms I had developed for each character.

The transition had to be immediate. That preparation took much longer than simply learning the lines. A George Bailey monologue is one thing, with the best Jimmy Stewart impression I can muster, but switching back and forth in a George and Mary dialogue requires even more practice.

The script by Steve Murray was written such that I was also the narrator, and I could use my own voice for that and set up a situation for both George and Mary or George with Mr. Potter. As Nick the Bartender, I was Sheldon Leonard performing as Nick. I tried my best to speak like Mr. Leonard for Nick and like Jimmy Stewart as George. I created my version of voices for all the other characters.

With George and Mary scenes, I could stand up straight as both characters, look up for the height difference when I was Mary and slightly downward for George. I would angle my body and/or head toward that particular person my character was speaking to. I didn't have to go back and forth from left to right in my stance, but just stand or sit in the same place while looking down or up, and to the left or right. If Potter and George were arguing, Potter was always in an office chair, doubling as a wheelchair at that moment. If it was older George talking to Mr. Potter at Potter's office, I would stay in the same chair on the same side of the desk, looking toward the audience. I would slump as Potter and sit up straighter as George.

I had acquired various set pieces for the many scenes of this play about a favorite movie. In the last week before opening night, we streamlined my furniture to just three pieces. On stage left was a shell of a desk. A bench from my late mother's front porch was on stage right. In the center and upstage, we had placed a step stool or library chair. These three pieces of furniture were the magic that made everything come together for the set.

The desk would represent the Bailey Building and Loan, but it also would be the desk in Mr. Potter's office. In another scene, it was the sundry counter at Mr. Gower's drug store. It was the piano where Janie practiced her music for the party that Christmas Eve. Turn it up on its side, and it's the bar at Martini's Lounge.

The library chair would serve as the stairs at Mary's house, but also the staircase and entire house of 320 Sycamore. This was the old, abandoned house that Mary later turned into the future Bailey residence. And since it was a library chair, it was converted to a regular chair when necessary. I would turn the top half over on itself to make the chair. That could be a seat for George after he paced back and forth outside the home of Mary Hatch, in his poor attempts at wooing her. Later, turned at an angle, I could be Ernie sitting in the front seat of his cab, or George and Mary in the back seat on the way to their honeymoon that didn't happen. I could lean forward as George or sit up and glance back at George as Ernie through the imaginary rearview mirror.

Mom's bench was my favorite transformation piece. In the beginning, it was the bench on the Bailey's front porch. Without moving it, later it becomes Zuzu's sick bed. Then, when George stumbles out of Martini's Bar, he heads to Zuzu's bed and Ma Bailey's porch, then I would turn Mama's bench around to the audience so that the seat was away from them. At that exact moment, it became the bridge where George believes the insurance policy in his pocket is the only way to solve his problem and save his family.

Standing at the bridge, the narrator tells the audience what George is considering as he looks down at the icy, black water that rushes toward the falls that give the town its name. But the bridge is also where Clarence jumps in the river for George to save him. And it is the same bridge George goes to in Pottersville to ask God to let him live again.

I cannot take credit for the multiple transitions of set pieces. I first saw this technique used in *King Lear* at McGlohon Theater in Charlotte. A throne became a table and then a cart. As I write this story more than a year after our production, I also see how I copied these transformation ideas from something else.

Prayers! They may not be the transforming techniques, but they certainly are the vehicle, and God is the source. We talk to Him through our prayers, and He answers through thoughts, feelings, scripture, and also in my case, through actions of other people . . . or perhaps through a movie, play, or song.

God answered my prayers every step of the way in this endeavor. He sent me a loving wife who believed in me, my best friend, Josh, who helped me craft this huge challenge and directed me, Dwight who helped me rehearse, and Caleb, who secured the venue and helped us package what we had in order to work best. That night was the most fun I ever had on stage. Two years of preparation made me see how God provides and how He never leaves us.

George yells at Mary, "Everything's wrong! You call this a happy family? Why did we have to have all these kids?" Attitude and perspective are sometimes perceived as the same or at least similar. Attitude is a settled way of thinking or feeling about someone or something. Perspective is a point of view, a particular attitude or way of regarding something.

George's life is crashing down around him, and he has become desperate. He had become somewhat bitter through the years, having to make sacrifices for others. Perhaps he lost sight of what he truly loved and what was most important. It took a glimpse from an angel to see what the world might be like if he had never been born. A different perspective and a positive attitude definitely helps.

All through this book, I have told my true-life stories and how I believe the townspeople of Bedford Falls felt and believed. Perhaps, the only person I can actually judge is myself. Through the one-person show of *This Wonderful Life* by Steve Murray and through writing these true stories in this book, I see how I've changed through the years.

Not just changing from bad to good, but I was innocent like young George with a good heart changing to a man who sometimes did the right thing in the right way for the right reasons but who sometimes failed miserably, then to a person who turned his back on God when life's struggles and blows seemed too hard. Fortunately, Papa never left me or gave up on me. I always knew we never had the next day promised to us, but I have to do right by the Lord and His grace for his many gifts and blessings. I'm not trying to be better than anyone else. I am simply trying to be a better man than I was yesterday. I need to be less like me and more like Jesus.

Clearly, my heavenly Father is not finished with me yet. Just as my earthly father loved me, cared for me, provided for me and wanted the best for me, so does He. Just as I wanted my dad to be proud of me, I want to live the way Jesus taught me, not to earn favor but to show my gratitude, love, and obedience. I want to be a service and help to others who struggle like me.

Transformers

The last three stories were repeats in a way, about Mother, Denise, and the play. They are the three loves of my life. Someone may say I shouldn't have been redundant. I say it wasn't redundant enough and hasn't scratched the surface of what all three have meant to me. My relationships with all three were exponentially better because of Jesus. As I strive to walk closer with him, everything else comes into perspective and in His glory.

> *Don't copy the behavior and customs of this world, but let God transform you into a new person by changing the way you think. Then you will learn to know God's will for you, which is good and pleasing and perfect.* (Romans 12:2)

> *So all of us who have had that veil removed can see and reflect the glory of the Lord. And the Lord—who is the Spirit—makes us more and more like him as we are changed into his glorious image.* (2 Corinthians 3:18)

> *In his kindness God called you to share in his eternal glory by means of Christ Jesus. So after you have suffered a little while, he will restore, support, and strengthen you, and he will place you on a firm foundation.* (1 Peter 5:10)

> *Search me, O God, and know my heart; test me and know my anxious thoughts. Point out anything in me that offends you, and lead me along the path of everlasting life.* (Psalm 139:23–24)

> *May the Lord lead your hearts into a full understanding and expression of the love of God and the patient endurance that comes from Christ.* (2 Thessalonians 3:5)

But to all who believed him and accepted him, he gave the right to become children of God. They are reborn—not with a physical birth resulting from human passion or plan, but a birth that comes from God. (John 1:12–13)

Cues to Clues to Truths

#50 Abba gives us the power to become the Children of God.

This new birth, not of human effort, brings change to our lives. We are a part of God's family, and He allows us to receive His many blessings.

"Attaboy, Clarence!" by Greg Clark Noir Art

It's a Wonderful Life– Character List

George Bailey—We see George as a young boy and an adult. Jimmy Stewart played the adult role. George saves his younger brother from drowning when they were boys, and he prevents Mr. Gower from accidentally poisoning a sick child. He always wants to see the world and build skyscrapers and bridges. George never wants to work at his father's Building and Loan but through a series of events, he ends up doing just that. He becomes a little cynical through the years, yet always helping others, doing the right thing, and sacrificing his dreams for the needs of everyone else.

Mary Bailey—We see her as a child, too. Donna Reed played Mary as an adult. She always loved Bedford Falls and George Bailey. The romantic Mary wanted to live in the old Granville house on 320 Sycamore. When she and George marry, she embraces everything that happens within being a wonderful wife and mother for her family, turning an old, empty house into a honeymoon cottage in a few hours, and rallying to save her family on Christmas Eve. Some even think Mary is the true hero of the story, and I would agree.

Clarence Oddbody—Played by Henry Travers, Clarence is George's guardian angel. On the night George is in trouble, Clarence is selected to save George. He is taught about how George helped people but never got to live out his dreams. Clarence has failed to earn his angel wings for hundreds of years, and he prepares to help George see that he truly has a wonderful life.

Harry Bailey—Harry is the younger brother of George Bailey. When they are young, he and George's friends go sledding. He falls through the ice and his big brother saves his life. Later, he becomes a football star, college graduate, pilot in World War II, and earns the Medal of Honor for saving men on a transport ship.

Peter Bailey—Peter is George and Harry's father. He started the Bailey Brothers Building and Loan with his brother, Billy. He sincerely wanted to help people in their town build their own homes and make something of themselves.

Ma Bailey—Played by Beulah Bondi, she is the mother of George and Harry Bailey. She helps George see that Mary Hatch is interested in him and encourages him to find love. In the Pottersville sequence, she is a bitter, grieving woman without George in her life.

Uncle Billy—Played by Thomas Mitchell, Billy Bailey helps his brother at the Bailey Brothers Building and Loan, and later his nephew upon Peter's death. He is a likable guy but a poor businessman. He has a bad memory and drinks a bit.

Annie the Maid—Annie is George and Harry Bailey's family's maid.

Henry Potter—Played by Lionel Barrymore, Mr. Potter is the wealthiest and meanest man in Bedford Falls. He wants to take control of the Building and Loan and tries to destroy it. Uncle Billy accidentally loses a large deposit which Potter steals, setting trouble in motion.

Ruth Dakin Bailey—Harry comes home from college with his wife, Ruth. Harry's new father-in-law gives him a job with his company. George, then realizes that Harry won't be taking over the Building and Loan, and he is still stuck in Bedford Falls.

Violet Bick—Violet had a crush on George as a child. As an adult, she is quite flirtatious. George helps her financially, but only as a friend and a person in need.

Mr. Gower—Mr. Gower owns the drugstore where George works as a boy. Terribly upset and grieving after his son dies of the flu, he mistakenly puts poison in the pill bottle for a sick child. George believes something is wrong and doesn't deliver the pills. Mr. Gower slaps his ear for disobeying him, but later becomes so thankful when he discovers his mistake.

Mr. Martini—Mr. Martini owns a bar in Bedford Falls. George helps him and his wife buy a home. He is so grateful for Mary and George and thinks of them as his dear friends. He is one of the many people praying for George on that fateful Christmas Eve.

Pete Bailey—He is George and Mary's oldest child, named after George's father. On that Christmas Eve, he is trying to write the Christmas story and needs help in spelling certain words.

Janie Bailey—Janie is George and Mary's older daughter. She practices "Hark! The Herald Angels Sing" on the piano for the Christmas Eve party.

Tommy Bailey—Cute Tommy Bailey is the youngest child of George and Mary Bailey. "Excuse me. I burped."

Zuzu Bailey—Zuzu may be a nickname instead of her real name, but it is believed it came from the cookie, Zu Zu Ginger Snaps. She catches a cold because she was given a flower at school, and doesn't want to button her coat for fear of crushing it. Zuzu has a touching scene with her father when she is sick and wants to continue looking at her flower rather than rest. He hides the loose petals to pretend he is fixing it for his daughter.

Sam Wainwright — As a child and an adult, Sam's catch phrase is "Hee Haw!" He dated Mary some, but she was more interested in George. Sam went to college and earned a fortune in plastics. Sam is wealthy like Potter but at the end of the movie, he advances George over three times what he needs.

Mrs. Hatch — We don't see much of Mary Hatch's mother in the movie, but we get the feeling she would rather her daughter marry the wealthy Sam Wainwright.

Bert — Bert is the cop and is good friends with George and Ernie. He helps Ernie tape travel posters over the windows George and Mary had broken years ago, to make a honeymoon cottage for the newlyweds on their wedding day.

Ernie — Ernie Bishop is the local cab driver. He is a good friend of George's. He drives George around several times in the movie. He has a very unhappy life in Pottersville.

Franklin and Joseph — They are the two senior angels teaching Clarence about his new assignment on earth.

Nick the bartender — Nick is the bartender at Martini's Lounge, and is a pretty nice guy. However, in Pottersville, Nick owns the bar that should be Martini's and is miserable and rude.

Mr. and Mrs. Welch — Mrs. Welch is Zuzu's teacher who gave her a flower for a prize at school. Zuzu doesn't want to crush it so she doesn't button her coat and catches a cold. She is sick but just wants to gaze at her flower, that loses petals and asks her father to fix it. Her father scolds Mrs. Welch over the phone for letting Zuzu catch a cold. Later at the bar, Mr. Welch punches George for upsetting his wife.

Sheriff—The sheriff has to present a warrant for George's arrest, on the matter of the missing eight thousand dollars. It was Uncle Billy's fault and Mr. Potter's deception, but George would be the one who would spend time in prison if the money wasn't recovered.

Bank Examiner—Mr. Carter is the bank examiner who checks on the finances of the Bailey Brothers Building and Loan on Christmas Eve. In the middle of his audit, Uncle Billy loses eight thousand dollars.

Freddie—He is played by Carl Switzer, who was Alfalfa in the original *The Little Rascals* series. In the movie, he's the one who uncovers the swimming pool under the dance floor because he is jealous that George dances with Mary at the high school dance.

Marty Hatch—Marty is Mary's brother and a childhood friend to George. At the dance, he asks George to dance with his sister.

Mr. Partridge—He is the high school principal who chaperones the dance and ends up jumping into the swimming pool when everyone else does.

Tom—Tom is the Bailey Building and Loan customer who, on the day of the bank run, wants his entire sum of two hundred forty-two dollars. He wouldn't settle for just a few dollars like the others to get by temporarily. His full withdrawal accounts for more than ten percent of what George and Mary were sacrificing from their honeymoon savings.

Mrs. Davis—After the run on the bank, this sweet lady asks for only seventeen dollars and fifty cents to get through the crisis of the bank run.

It's a Wonderful Life—Summary

Many love *It's a Wonderful Life*. Many know a little bit about it, and still others have never seen it. If a character list doesn't give you enough background, try this brief summary.

On Christmas Eve, 1945, George Bailey is contemplating suicide. Prayers go up for him from friends and family of Bedford Falls, New York. In heaven, two senior angels prepare Clarence to go to earth to rescue George. They give the guardian angel, who has yet to earn his wings, a little background on George Bailey.

When he was twelve, George saved the life of his younger brother, Harry, who fell through the ice in a sledding accident. Some months later, when working for Mr. Gower, the pharmacist, George saves the life of a sick boy in the neighborhood as well as that of his boss. Mr. Gower was upset upon the death of his son from the Spanish Flu, and mistakenly put poison in the prescription bottle for the young boy.

George always wants to explore the world, come back and go to college, then build skyscrapers, bridges, and airfields. Something always seems to prevent these dreams from coming true. He goes to his brother's school dance where he reunites with Mary Hatch, his friend Marty's younger sister. They have a nice evening dancing and swimming, singing and talking. George is called away by Harry and their uncle. Their father dies that night after a stroke, and George helps run his father's business for a few months. He has to continue because Mr. Potter tries to shut down the Building and Loan.

Another time, Harry comes home from college with his wife, Ruth. George had hoped Harry would run the family business and let him go to college. The richest and meanest man in town, Mr. Potter, still wants to destroy the Building and Loan.

Mary had always cared for George, even as a child, and one night George finds himself calling on her. She plays a record of "Buffalo Gals" which was the song they sang walking away from the dance. George thinks she is teasing him. Mary's mother wants her to marry wealthy Sam Wainwright, but George and Mary soon get married, much to Mrs. Hatch's sadness.

On the way to the train station to begin their honeymoon. They see people going to the bank. There has been a stock market crash and people want to get their money right away. George and Mary go to the Bailey Building and Loan and find several people waiting outside with the door locked. Mary hands over the two thousand dollars intended for their honeymoon.

They try to use the money to get their customers through this crisis temporarily. Tom insists on getting all his money back. In so doing, he takes two hundred and forty-two dollars and leaves less than ninety percent for everyone else. Mrs. Davis doesn't take forty or twenty dollars, but only asks for seventeen dollars and fifty cents. George is so moved that he gives her a big kiss.

George receives a call from Mary to come home. While he and the others were struggling to keep the Building and Loan afloat, Mary turned the abandoned home at 320 Sycamore where they once made wishes and broke windows on the night of the school dance. Bert and Ernie tape travel posters over the broken windows and sing "I Love You Truly" for the newlyweds.

George continues to help others in Bedford Falls, often giving money out of his own pocket, but ultimately following his father's philosophy to help their fellow citizens have a decent roof over their heads, It seems Mr. Potter got wealthier while George stayed the same. He forgets how special everything is that Mary and he had built together and also had been blessed with four beautiful children, Peter, Janie, Zuzu, and Tommy.

It's a Wonderful Life—Summary

When the senior angels have Clarence and all of us up to speed on the life of George Bailey, we learn brother Harry Bailey has been awarded the Medal of Honor. Uncle Billy goes to the bank to deposit eight thousand dollars for the business. He cannot pass up the opportunity to gloat to Mr. Potter over his nephew and in the pleasure of the moment and his forgetfulness, he mistakenly folds the deposit into Mr. Potter's newspaper. He notices soon but can't recall what he did with the money.

It's bad enough that the bank examiner showed up on Christmas Eve, but now there is a large sum missing, and Uncle Billy and George can't find it anywhere. George goes to Mr. Potter for help, and even though he has the lost money in his possession, Potter doesn't confess.

Distraught, George goes home to his family. Mary is decorating the Christmas tree. Pete is writing the Christmas story and needs help with words like frankincense and hallelujah. Janie is practicing the piano for the party that night. Tommy asked to be excused for his burp, and Zuzu is upstairs, sick in bed. George has a tender moment with Zuzu and pretends to glue the fallen petals on the flower she got from her teacher. She didn't want to crush it so she didn't button her coat and caught a cold.

Soon though, George is snapping at Mary, the other children, and Zuzu's teacher, Mrs. Welch, when she called to check on her. He destroys his model bridges and buildings, and stumbles out into the night. He goes to Mr. Martini's bar and prays, although he admits he isn't a praying man. Mr. Welch is there and punches him in the face, George believes that is God's answer to his prayer.

George crashes his car into a tree in the snow, and goes to the bridge over the river. Here, he grasps his insurance policy and contemplates jumping into the river. At that moment, Clarence jumps in instead so George will save him rather than take his own life.

Clarence seems strange to George, not believing he is actually his guardian angel. When George wishes he'd never been born, Clarence decides how to open George's eyes, perhaps because of his favorite book, *Tom Sawyer* by Mark Twain, he carries with him. In that book, Tom witnesses his own funeral. Clarence attempts to show George what life would be like without him in it.

He is no longer in Bedford Falls, and the now miserable town is called Pottersville. Nick owns the bar instead of Martini but isn't friendly. George can't understand why Mr. Gower doesn't recognize him. Grumpy Nick throws George and Clarence out of his bar. Mr. Gower did time in prison because George wasn't there the day his son died. Clarence takes George to a cemetery where George learns his brother died in that sledding accident. He argues with Clarence that Harry won the Medal of Honor for saving the men on a transport ship. His angel explains that Harry wasn't there to save them because George wasn't there to save Harry.

George leaves Clarence to find his family, but Mary doesn't recognize him. George returns to the bridge where he saved Clarence. All the while in Pottersville, there wasn't any new snowfall as in Bedford Falls. George begs Clarence to help him and prays to God to let him live again. It begins snowing on the bridge. Bert the cop recognizes George although he didn't in Pottersville. George is elated to discover his mouth is bleeding again from Mr. Welch's punch and that Zuzu's petals are once again in his pocket.

George is so happy he is back in his hometown. He may be going to jail, but at least he will still have his beautiful family. He shouts "Merry Christmas" to the movie house, the old Building and Loan, and to Bedford Falls' wealthy curmudgeon, Henry Potter. He replies to George by telling him the sheriff and bank examiner are waiting for him.

Excited to be home again in that drafty old barn, George hugs his children. God answered another prayer in that little Zuzu hasn't a smitch of temperature! Mary enters, so joyful to find George at home.

She is followed by half the town of Bedford Falls who make contributions. Mary and Uncle Billy have been collecting money from neighbors who want to help. Harry arrives, straight from his Medal of Honor ceremony in Washington and toasts his big brother, George, "the richest man in town." Ernie the cabbie reads a telegram from Sam Wainwright that he is advancing George twenty-five thousand dollars. The sheriff tears up the warrant, and George sees Clarence's copy of *Tom Sawyer* in the basket with an inscription inside. "Dear George, Remember no man is a failure who has friends. Love, Clarence."

Just then, Zuzu hears a bell ring on the Christmas tree and informs them that her teacher says every time a bell rings an angel gets his wings. "Attaboy, Clarence! Attaboy!"

Acknowledgments

I wish to thank the following people for their artistry and contributions to this book:

Bill Vinson, my creative writing teacher, who encouraged me to explore poetry and realize for myself that I do really like it and to expand on what meager writing skills I have by being courageous enough to put the first word on paper and follow that with strings of others that hopefully make sense.

Greg Clark and Greg Clark Noir Art for illustrations included in these pages that capture the magic of *It's a Wonderful Life*

Shelby Greene Cox and Over the Moon Photography for not only shooting images of my family and certain possessions, but treating every living being with dignity and grace as if her own, and every article with detail and respect as though they were also priceless

Bibliography

3:10 to Yuma. Directed by Delmer Daves, Columbia Pictures, 1957.

20,000 Leagues Under the Sea. Directed by Richard Fleischer, Walt Disney Studios Motion Pictures, 1954.

Apollo 13. Directed by Ron Howard, Universal Pictures, 1995.

A Christmas Carol. Directed by Clive Donner, Entertainment Partners Ltd., 1984.

A League of Their Own. Directed by Penny Marshall, Columbia Pictures, 1992.

Baum, L. Frank. *The Marvelous Land of Oz (Illustrated).* 1904.

Baum, L. Frank. *The Wizard of Oz.* Adapted by Anne Coulter Martens, Dramatic Publishing Company. 1963.

Berlin, Irving. "This is the Army, Mr. Jones." *This is the Army.* 1942.

Bibb, Eric. "The Cape." *Troubadour Live.* Telarc, 2011.

"Bible Search and Study Tools—Blue Letter Bible." www.blueletter-bible.org.

Burns, Robert. "Auld Lang Syne." 1788.

Capurro, Giovanni. "O Sole Mio." 1898.

Cast Away. Directed by Robert Zemeckis, 20th Century Studios, 2000.

Cole, Edwin Louis. *Maximized Manhood: A Guide to Family Survival.* New Kensington, PA, Whitaker House, 2015.

Danniel, Erika. "50 Top Promises of God in the Bible." https://christian.net, October 4, 2021.

DeVille, Willy, and Mark Knopfler. "Storybook Love." *The Princess Bride (Soundtrack),* Warner Brothers Records, 1987.

Dickens, Charles. *A Christmas Carol.* Adapted by Beth Woodard and Mark Allen Woodard, Foothills Performing Arts' production, 2011.

Dickens, Charles, and Gustave Doré. *Charles Dickens' A Christmas Carol: With 45 Lost Gustave Doré Engravings (1861) and 130 Other Victorian Illustrations; Introduction by Dan Malan.* St. Louis, MCE Publishing Company, 1996.

Driving Miss Daisy. Directed by Bruce Beresford, Warner Brothers, 1989.

Elwes, Cary, and Joe Layden. *As You Wish: Inconceivable Tales from the Making of The Princess Bride.* New York, NY, Atria Books, 2016.

Every Man's Bible NLT. Carol Stream, IL, Tyndale House Publishers, Inc., 2014.

Finding Nemo. Directed by Andrew Stanton, Walt Disney Pictures, 2003.

Forrest Gump. Directed by Robert Zemeckis, Paramount Pictures, 1994.

Four Weddings and a Funeral. Directed by Mike Newell, Universal Pictures, 1994.

Gilmore, Patrick. "When Johnny Comes Marching Home." 1863.

Groundhog Day. Directed by Harold Ramis, Columbia Pictures, 1993.

Hodges, John. "Buffalo Gals." 1844.

"How to Board a Boat with Confidence (in 5 Steps)." Written by Shawn Buckles, *Improve Sailing*, improvesailing.com/tips/how-to-board-a-boat-with-confidence-in-5-steps.

Hubbard, Ray Wylie. "Snake Farm." *Snake Farm*. Sustain Records, 2006.

It's a Wonderful Life. Directed by Frank Capra, Liberty Films Inc., 1946.

Jacobs-Bond, Carrie. "I Love You Truly." *Seven Songs as Unpretentious as the Wild Rose*. 1901.

Johnson, James P. "Charleston." 1923.

Jolson, Al, et al. "Avalon." 1920.

Jones, Jessie, et al. *Christmas Belles*. New York, Dramatists Play Service, 2007.

King, Charles E. "Song of the Islands (Na Lei O Hawaii)." 1915.

King, Stephen. *Misery*. 1987.

King, Stephen. *The Green Mile*. 1996.

Lacourrege, Megan. *My Sibling Still: for those who've lost a sibling to miscarriage, stillbirth or infant death*. R. R. Bowker, 2019.

Lee, Harper. *To Kill a Mockingbird*. J. B. Lippincott & Company, 1960.

Lopez, Robert, et al. *Avenue Q, the Musical: The Complete Book and Lyrics of the Broadway Musical*. Milwaukee, WI, Applause Theatre & Cinema Books, 2010.

Mary Poppins. Directed by Robert Stevenson, Walt Disney Studios Motion Pictures, 1964.

Mendelssohn, Felix. "Wedding March." 1842.

Michael. Directed by Nora Ephron, Warner Brothers, 1996.

Miles, Charles Austin. "In the Garden." 1912.

Mills, Quinton. "He Never Left Me." *Live…Uprising & Best of Quinton Mills*. Better Way Records, 2008.

Morton, Jelly Roll. "King Porter Stomp." 1923.

Mula, Tom. *Jacob Marley's Christmas Carol*. Dramatists Play Service, Inc., 2004.

Multiplicity. Directed by Harold Ramis, Columbia Pictures, 1996.

Murray, Steve, et al. *This Wonderful Life*. Playscripts, 2010.

Netsky, Aaron. "The Tangled Origin Stories for the Term 'Green Room.'" www.onstageblog.com, November 30, 2017.

Offenbach, Jacques, music, and Francesco Maria Scala, introduction as first director of the Marine Corps Band, (Lyrics of unknown origin). "Marines' Hymn," United States Marine Corps, 1919.

Olcott, Chauncy. "My Wild Irish Rose." Historic Sheet Music Collection. 1846.

O'Neill, Owen, and Dave Johns. *The Shawshank Redemption*. Dramatists Play Service, 2019.

Parton, Dolly. "Coat of Many Colors." *Coat of Many Colors*. RCA Victor, 1971.

Peanuts, Created by Charles Shulz, www.peanuts.com.

Pink Floyd. "Another Brick in the Wall." *The Wall*. Columbia Records, 1979.

Rooney, Tom. *Flaming Idiots*. Samuel French, Inc., 1993.

Roxanne. Directed by Fred Schepisi, Columbia Pictures, 1987.

Saving Private Ryan. Directed by Steven Spielberg, Paramount Pictures, 1998.

Scott, Walter. *Ivanhoe*. 1904.

Scrooge (United Kingdom), (Released as *A Christmas Carol* in the United States). Directed by Brian Desmond Hurst, Renown Pictures, 1951.

Sergel, Christopher, and Harper Lee. *To Kill a Mockingbird: A Full-Length Play*. Woodstock, IL, Dramatic Publishing Company, 1970.

Shakespeare, William. *King Lear*. New York, NY. Simon & Schuster Paperbacks, 2015.

Sherman, Robert B., and Richard M. Sherman. "A Spoonful of Sugar." *Mary Poppins (Soundtrack),* Walt Disney Productions, 1964.

Sherrod, Robert. *Tarawa: The Story of a Battle*. Duell, Sloan, and Pearce, 1944.

Shortcuts. Directed by Robert Altman, New Line Cinema, 1993.

Sleepless in Seattle. Directed by Nora Ephron, TriStar Pictures, 1993.

Snow White and the Seven Dwarfs. Directed by Perce Pearce, et al, Walt Disney Productions, 1937.

Sousa, John Philip. "The Stars and Stripes Forever." 1896.

Spencer's Mountain. Directed by Delmer Daves, Warner Brothers, 1963.

St. Elmo's Fire. Directed by Joel Schumacher, Columbia Pictures, 1985.

Talking Heads "Burning Down the House." *Speaking in Tongues,* Sire Records, 1983.

Taylor, Jane. "Twinkle, Twinkle, Little Star." 1806.

Teague, Sanford. "Boston is Youngest Black Pastor in Alex." www.taylorsvilletimes.com. February 9, 2022.

The Bells of St. Mary's. Directed by Leo McCarey, RKO Radio Pictures, 1945.

The Godfather Part III. Directed by Francis Ford Coppola, Paramount Pictures, 1990.

The Green Mile. Directed by Frank Darabont, Warner Brothers, 1999.

The Incredible Mr. Limpet. Directed by Arthur Lubin, Warner Brothers, 1964.

The Last Samurai. Directed by Edward Zwick, Warner Brothers, 2003.

The Little Rascals (also known as *Our Gang*), Created by Hal Roach, Directed by Robert F. McGowan, King World Productions, 1922 to 1944.

The Princess Bride. Directed by Rob Reiner, 20th Century Fox, 1987.

The Shining. Directed by Stanley Kubrick, Warner Brothers, 1980.

The Waltons, Created by Earl Hamner, Jr., 1972 to 1981, CBS, www.the-waltons.com.

The Wizard of Oz. Directed by Victor Fleming, Metro-Goldwyn-Mayer, 1939.

Twain, Mark. *The Adventures of Tom Sawyer.* Oxford, Oxford University Press, 1876.

Valée, Rudy & His Connecticut Yankees. "Vieni, Vieni." 1937.

Verne, Jules. *Twenty Thousand Leagues Under the Sea.* 1870.

Wade, John Francis. "O Come, All Ye Faithful." 1751.

Welch, Bob. *52 Little Lessons from It's a Wonderful Life.* Nashville, TN, Thomas Nelson, 2012.

Wesley, Charles, and George Whitefield. "Hark! The Herald Angels Sing." 1739.

White, Michael B. "It's a Wonderful Life." *It's a Wonderful Life.* Apple Music, 2009.

Willian, Michael. *The Essential It's a Wonderful Life: A Scene-By-Scene Guide to the Classic Film.* Chicago, IL, Chicago Review Press, 2006.